Copyright © 2008 A.D.A. EDITA Tokyo Co., Ltd.
3-12-14 Sendagaya, Shibuya-ku, Tokyo 151-0051, Japan
All rights reserved. No part of this publication may be reproduced,
stored in a retrieval system, or transmitted, in any form or by any means,
electronic, mechanical, photocopying, recording, or otherwise,
without permission in writing from the publisher.

Copyright of photographs
©2008 GA photographers

Logotype design: Gan Hosoya

Printed and bound in Japan

ISBN 978-4-87140-491-4 C1052

HOUSES IN
MEXICO

A.D.A. EDITA Tokyo

HOUSES IN MEXICO

Edited and Photographed by Yukio Futagawa

目次　　Contents

1章　Chapter 1
伝統的背景　Traditional Background

エッセイ：「メキシコ建築の視座」　　　　　　　　　　'A Vision of Mexican Architecture'
　　　　ホセ・ルイス・コルテス　10　Jose Luis Cortes

ベルナルド・ゴメス=ピメンタ, エンリケ・ノルテン　　**Bernardo Gomez-Pimienta, Enrique Norten**
　バイエ・デ・ブラボのアシエンダ改修計画　14　Salas-Basanni House

ホセ・ルイス・コルテス　　**Jose Luis Cortes**
　コルテス自邸　30　Cortes House

2章　Chapter 2
モダニズムの開花　Efflorescence of Modernism

エッセイ：「革命と変遷—　　　　　　　　　　　　　'Revolution and Evolution—
メキシコにおける近代住宅の興隆」　38　The Rise of the Modern House in Mexico'
　　　アレハンドロ・アプティロン　　　　　　　　　Alejandro Aptilon

ホアン・オゴルマン　　**Juan O'Gorman**
　ディエゴ・リベラとフリーダ・カーロの家／スタジオ　46　Diego Rivera and Frida Kahlo House-Studio
　オゴルマン自邸　56　Architect's House

ルイス・バラガン　　**Luis Barragán**
　バラガン自邸　62　Barragán House

マックス・ルートヴィヒ・チェット　　**Max Ludwig Cetto**
　チェット自邸　76　Cetto House

フランシスコ・アルティガス＆フェルナンド・ルナ　　**Francisco Artigas & Fernando Luna**
　ロハス・ハウス　82　Rojas House
　サン・アンヘルの住宅　86　House in San Angel

フランシスコ・アルティガス　　**Francisco Artigas**
　アルティガス自邸　90　Architect's House

フェルナンド・アルティガス, LAR／フェルナンド・ロメロ　　**Fernando Artigas, LAR/Fernando Romero**
　ビレイエス・ハウス　94　Virreyes House

ハイメ・オルティス・モナステリオ　　**Jaime Ortiz Monasterio**
　オブレゴン・ハウス　98　Obregon House

3章		Chapter 3
現代建築の成長		**Development of Contemporary Architecture**
エッセイ：「バラガン後のメキシコ現代住宅」		**'Contemporary Mexican Houses after Barragán'**
ミケール・アドリア	102	Miquel Adria
リカルド・レゴレッタ／レゴレッタ・アルキテクトス		**Ricard Legorreta/Legorreta Arquitectos**
バイエ・デ・ブラボの住宅	106	House in Valle de Bravo
南カリフォルニアの住宅	112	House in Southern California
ラ・コロラダ・ハウス	118	La Colorada House
レゴレッタ自邸	126	Ricardo Legorreta's House
カベルネ・ハウス	134	Casa Cabernet
エンリケ・ノルテン／TENアルキテクトス		**Enrique Norten/TEN Arquitectos**
ハウス'O'	142	House 'O'
ハウスR.R.	150	House R.R.
アルベルト・カラチ		**Alberto Kalach**
ネグロ・ハウス	158	Negro House
GGGハウス	168	GGG House
グルッポLBC		**Grupo LBC**
バイエ・デ・ブラボの住宅	176	Casa en Valle de Bravo
BGPアルキテクトゥーラ		**BGP Arquitectura**
ハウスGDL1	182	House GDL1
LCM／フェルナンド・ロメロ		**LCM/Fernando Romero**
イスタパの住宅	186	Ixtapa House
ミシェル・ルーキング		**Michel Rojkind**
Prハウス	192	Pr House
フェリペ・レアル		**Felipe Leal**
ガレアナ71	198	Galeana 71

Cover: Barragán House by Luis Barragán
Title pages: San Cristobal (House for Mr. and Mrs. Folke Egerstrom, horse pool, stable) by Luis Barragán
エッセイ和訳：菊池泰子（pp.10-13, pp.38-45），常石憲彦（pp.102-105）

El Babedero, Las Arboledas, 1959-62
Luis Barragán participated in the project in the mid 1950's to develop a new residential area in Las Arboledas district, which was still the suburbs of Mexico City at that time. It was El Bebedero, one of the three installations created as the symbols of the project, which was built at the eastern edge of the site. The water pool provided as a drinking fountain for horses is accompanied by blue and white wall surfaces to become the abstract monuments of the plaza space.

〈エル・ベベデーロ, ラス・アルボレーダス, 1959-62年〉
ルイス・バラガンは, 1950年代半ば, 当時メキシコ・シティの郊外であったラス・アルボレーダス地区に新しい住宅地を開発する計画に参加した。その計画のシンボルとしてつくられた三つの装置のうちの一つが, 敷地の東端につくられた, このエル・ベベデーロである。馬用の水飲み場としてつくられたこの水槽は, 青と白の壁面と合わせて広場の抽象的なモニュメントとなっている。

A Vision of Mexican Architecture
Jose Luis Cortes

メキシコ建築の視座
ホセ・ルイス・コルテス

Teotihuacan テオティワカン

Mexico is a country located in North America, surrounded on the west side by the Pacific sea, on the east by the Atlantic—within the Gulf of Mexico—, and by the Caribbean on the south; its neighbors down south are Guatemala and Belize, and shares a long border up north with the United States. Mexico's territory is two million square kilometers, divided in 32 states, with a population of 105 million people.

Mexico's Architectural History has been extremely rich throughout the centuries since the Pre-hispanic times, that is before the 16th century; but long before different cultures developed through several thousand years, mainly in the center and south of Mexico. These cultures, among many others, are the Olmecs in the Gulf of Mexico, the Mayans located in the south of Mexico and Central-America, the Mixtecs and Zapotecs in what nowadays is the State of Oaxaca, the Totonacs in the State of Veracruz, the Teotihuacans in the northern Valley of Mexico City, and the Aztecs in the place where Mexico's capital is located.

The Aztec's capital, Tenochtitlan, was surrounded by the Texcoco Lake, and when its people arrived at the Valley of Mexico in 1325, the different tribes occupying the land sent the Aztecs—who had arrived from the west of the country—to set up themselves in the center of the lake assuming they would not be able to survive; but the Aztecs were notorious for their warrior spirit and they not only built up Tenochtitlan and conquered the Valley of Mexico but the whole country, for almost 100 years, and managed to rule for another 100 years until the Spaniards arrived in 1519.

When the Spaniards landed they brought along with them an accumulation of diverse European cultures, and architecturally speaking they carried a strong Arabic influence with reminiscences of Roman, Greek, Fenitian, and many other architectures.

During the 16th century the Spaniards built in Mexico nearly 600 churches, convents, and quite a few cathedrals—spread around the country—trying to promote the catholic religion; most of them were built on top of the Pre-hispanic ceremonial centers, enriched with wonderful handcrafted Indian labor and magnificent stones for the pyramids. Its artisans and masons were greatly qualified for building these impressive and majestic religious buildings designed by the Spanish architects.

During the 16th, 17th, 18th, and 19th century, the Viceroyalty period, most cities were developed on the basis of what was designated "The dream of an order", established by Charles V and Phillip II throughout a period that runs from 1524 to 1574; with that dream in mind they created 350 cities in America. The basic principle of this city's layout was a main square where the religious and civic authorities were sited, and all streets ran parallel in both directions: north south bound, and east to west. The Mexicans loved this pattern because, from an urban point of view, it resembled the concepts of order of the Pre-hispanic centers, except for

メキシコは北米大陸に位置し，西を太平洋，東を大西洋が流れ込むメキシコ湾，南をカリブ海に囲まれ，南隣りはグアテマラとベリーズ，北隣りはアメリカ合衆国と長い国境を接している。メキシコの国土は200万平方キロ，32の州に分かれ，人口は1億500万人である。

メキシコにおける建築の歴史は，16世紀以前のプレ・ヒスパニック時代からの数世紀を通して非常に豊かなものであるが，遥か昔，数千年の間には，主にメキシコの中央部と南部に様々な文化が栄えてきた。これらの文化には，メキシコ湾岸のオルメカ，メキシコ南部と中央アメリカに位置したマヤ，現在はオアハカ州であるミステクとサポテカ，ベラクルス州のトトナック，メキシコ・シティの北にある渓谷のテオティワカン，そしてメキシコの首都が位置する場所に栄えたアステカがある。

アステカの首都テノチティトゥランは，テスココ湖に囲まれていた。1325年，アステカ族がこの国の西からメキシコ渓谷に到着したとき，この土地に住んでいた他の部族はアステカ族をテスココ湖の中心へと送った。生き延びることができないだろうと考えたためである。しかしアステカ族はその戦闘的な精神でよく知られ，テノチティトゥランを建設し，メキシコ渓谷ばかりでなく国全体をほぼ100年の間に征服し，1519年にスペイン人が到着するまでさらに100年間，統治したのである。

スペイン人が上陸したとき，彼らは多種多様なヨーロッパ文化の集積を持ち込み，建築的に言えば，ローマ，ギリシャ，フェニキア，その他多くの建築の遺産と共にアラビアの強い影響をもたらした。16世紀中に，スペイン人は，カトリック信仰を広めるために，メキシコ中に600近くの教会，修道院，かなりの数のカテドラルを建設した。それらのほとんどは，プレ・ヒスパニック時代につくられた，インディオの見事な手仕事とピラミッドの素晴らしい石積みで飾られた祭壇の上に建てられた。その職人たちや石工たちは，スペイン人建築家によって設計された厳粛で荘重な宗教建築を建てるのにまさに適任であった。

16〜19世紀にわたるスペインによる副王統治の時代，ほとんどの都市は，カルロス5世とフェリペ2世によって1524年から1574年を通して確立された「理想の統治」を明示する構想によって開発された。その理想を胸に，彼らはアメリカ大陸に350の都市をつくりあげた。こうした都市のレイアウトの基本原則は，宗教施設と公共機関を中心の広場に置き，南北，東西の両方向にすべての道が平行して走るものであった。メキシコ人はこの構成を好んだ。というのは，全く異なる地形状況に開発された鉱山の町を別にすれば，都市の視点からみると，それはプレ・ヒスパニック時代の中心の秩序を構成するコンセプトに似ていたからである。金銀の鉱山は，スペイン人が，豪華な内部装飾が施された厳威に満ちた建築のある美しい歴史地区をつくりあげるのに役立った。

都市の外側の田園地帯では，広大な土地が農業や牧畜を目的に開発され，「アシエンダ（大農場）」というコンセプトの下，農場主が住む主屋の素晴らしいメキシ

A series of houses for San Angel by Manuel Parra
マヌエル・パラ設計，サン・アンヘルの一連の住宅

Zocalo (Plaza de la Constitucion) and La Catedral Metropolitana, Mexico City
ソカロ広場とメトロポリタン大聖堂，メキシコ・シティ

the mining towns that were developed in quite different topographic conditions. The gold and silver mines helped the Spaniards build beautiful historic centers with superb architecture, enriched with a luxurious interior decoration.

Outside the cities, in the rural areas, large extensions of land were developed for agricultural and cattle raising purposes, and organized under the concept of "Haciendas", many of them amazingly original due to the great Mexican architecture in the owner's main house, provided with plenty of rooms for family and visitors around several patios, and surrounded by beautiful gardens, green houses, barns, stables, and shops for the people working in the "Hacienda" where they received their salaries and bought basic products on credit; many of these Haciendas had superb adjacent chapels.

There were many of these Mexican "Haciendas" around the country devoted to different economic activities such as coffee plantations, wine production, sugar mills, cattle raising, tobacco growing, all kinds of agriculture, and many other purposes; most of them were erected during the 17th, 18th, and 19th centuries and were developed as great examples of architecture where one can recognize the syncretism between Spanish and Mexican culture.

As you may have guessed many contemporary architects have been inspired and nurtured by the Pre-hispanic and the Viceroyalty architecture.

When in 1810 Mexico declared its independence from Spain most Mexican architects were graduated from San Carlos Academy, in Mexico City. This Academy was founded in 1781 and considered the main school for painters, sculptors, and architects in America, and its uniqueness came from educating architects and artists in the same place. A great architect that influenced the Academy was Manuel Tolsa, born in Valencia, Spain, and who also designed some of Mexico City's most important Colonial buildings.

During the 19th and part of the 20th century San Carlos Academy became extremely prominent and many foreign architects from Italy and France were involved in different projects around the country. At the end of the 19th century president Porfirio Diaz began building the Fine Arts Palace and the Post Office building with the help of Adamo Boari, a well known Italian architect at the time. The whole railroad system was built with excellent architecture along the stations, and lots of markets and theaters in different cities are still good examples of that period.

The Mexican Revolution broke out in 1910, and its struggles throughout the country killed one million from a population of 10 million people; the urbanization process began soon after the Revolution with the emigration from the rural to the urban areas, having its strongest impact in Mexico City's area, capital of the country, also called Federal District.

After 1930 Mexico developed what was called Post–revolutionary ar-

コ建築のおかげで，その多くが驚くほど独創的なものとなっている。主屋は，いくつものパティオを囲むようにして，家族や来客のために多くの部屋を備え，美しい庭や，温室，納屋，厩，そして「アシエンダ」で働く人々が給料を受け取り，つけで日常品を買える店が取り囲む。これらのアシエンダの多くには素晴らしい礼拝堂が隣接している。

国中に散在する，こうしたメキシコの「アシエンダ」の多くは，コーヒー農場，ワインの醸造所，砂糖工場，牧畜，煙草栽培，あらゆる種類の農産物，その他多くの目的を持つ様々な経済活動に充てられている。そのほとんどは17，18，19世紀につくられ，スペインとメキシコ両文化の重層構造を見ることのできる建築の壮大な例証として展開していった。

推察されるように，現代建築家の多くが，プレ・ヒスパニック建築と副王統治時代の建築から刺激を受け，育てられてきた。

1810年，メキシコがスペインからの独立を宣言したとき，ほとんどのメキシコ人建築家はメキシコ・シティのサン・カルロス美術学院を卒業していた。この美術学院は1781年に設立され，メキシコにおける画家，彫刻家，建築家のための主要な学校と考えられ，その特徴は，建築家とアーティストを同じ場所で教育することにあった。美術学院に影響を与えた優れた建築家は，スペインのバレンシアに生まれたマヌエル・トルサで，彼はまた，メキシコ・シティの最も重要なコロニアル建築をいくつか設計している。

19世紀全般と20世紀の一時期にかけて，サン・カルロス美術学院は非常に有名になり，イタリアやフランスから来訪した多くの外国人建築家が国中の様々なプロジェクトに関わった。19世紀末には，ポルフィリオ・ディアス大統領が，当時よく知られていたイタリア人建築家，アダモ・ボアリの助けを借りて美術宮殿と郵便局を建設し始めた。鉄道網全体が駅に沿った素晴らしい建築と共に建設され，様々な都市の数多くの市場や劇場は今もこの時代のよい実例となって残っている。

1910年，メキシコ革命が勃発し，国中で行われたその闘争により1千万の人口のうち，100万人が殺された。革命後まもなく，田舎から都市への人々の移動と共に都市化が始まり，その最も強い影響は首都であり，連邦区とも呼ばれるメキシコ・シティにもたらされた。

1930年以降，メキシコは，その非常にマッシヴな公共建築で知られる，いわゆる「革命後の建築」を発展させたが，しかしまたアール・デコの影響や，ル・コルビュジエの理論に啓発された「ディエゴ・リベラ／フリーダ・カーロ邸」を設計し建設したホアン・オゴルマン（1905-82年）のようなその他のスタイルも歓迎した。バウハウスも市のあちらこちらの合理主義者による多くのプロジェクトにとって参照の主要な対象であり，多くの建築家がこの運動に従った。

1940年からの数年間，メキシコ・シティは，メキシコの建築への対処において非常に独創的な，2人の特別に際立った建築家を持つことになる。一人はルイス・バラガン（1902-88年）であり，ハリスコ州の首都グアダラハラでエンジニアと

Satellite Towers by Luis Barragán and Mathias Goeritz (Queretaro Highway, Mexico City, 1957)
ルイス・バラガンとマティアス・ゲーリッツによる
サテライト・タワー（メキシコ・シティ，1957年）

Camino Real Hotel (Mexico City, 1968) conceived by Ricard Legorreta
リカルド・レゴレッタの構想による
カミノ・レアル・ホテル（メキシコ・シティ，1968年）

National Autonomous University of Mexico by Jan O'Gorman, Mario Pani, Enrique del Moral and others in 1950s
ホアン・オゴルマン，マリオ・パニ，エンリケ・デル・モラル等により1950年代につくられたメキシコ国立自治大学

chitecture, known for its very massive public buildings, but also welcomed Art Deco influences and other styles like Juan O'Gorman (1905-82)'s who designed and built 'Diego Rivera and Frida Kahlo's studio', inspired in Le Corbusier theories; the Bauhaus was also a reference point for many rationalist projects around the city, and a number of architects followed this movement.

In the years following 1940 Mexico City had two distinguished architects, among many others, quite original in their approach to Mexican architecture: Luis Barragán (1902-88), trained as an engineer in Guadalajara, capital of the State of Jalisco, and whose inspiration emanates from the old "Haciendas", where he was brought up; he designed superb contemporary homes full of Mexican brilliant colors; he was a friend of Chucho Reyes, a painter from his hometown, who moved to Mexico City and pushed him to use bright colors in his buildings. Another good friend of him was Mathias Goeritz, a sculptor born in Poland, that came to Mexico around those years and together with Barragán designed the 'Satellite Towers', an urban symbol of Mexico City. Barragán was awarded with the Pritzker Price.

The other original Mexican architect during that period was Manuel Parra (1911-97), trained in Architecture in San Carlos Academy, and who very soon began recycling old materials from demolished houses in the city's center and using those same materials in the new houses he designed for the suburbs of San Angel and Coyoacan, two villages used by the Spaniards in the Viceroyalty time as their second home, where they would grow fantastic fruit gardens to enjoy during their relaxation periods. He built more than a hundred houses using his great creativity to produce this unique spaces, unexpected to the eye's visitors, at low cost, and with reminiscences of the Spanish flavor, that also helped recover those neighborhood's urban image.

If we speak of the academic field, another architect that had a strong influence because of his books on *Theory of Architecture* was Jose Villagran Garcia (1901-82), whose buildings borne from his unparallel conceptions one can still visit.

At the beginning of the fifties Mexico City witnessed a boom of brilliant architecture: an example would be the 'Latinamerica Tower' and 'Mexico City's International Airport', designed by Augusto Alvarez, a rationalistic architect, the Iberoamerican University's first Dean of Architecture, also known for many other exceptional buildings. 'Mexico's Autonomous National University' campus was built in 1951 with the participation of more than 200 architects, a set of buildings recently considered as World Heritage by UNESCO; the outset of this University's open spaces clearly derives from the Pre-hispanic architecture.

The Museum of Anthropology, designed in the sixties by Pedro Ramirez Vazquez and Jorge Campuzano, is again a good example of ar-

して訓練され，そのひらめきのある発想は彼が育った場所である古い「アシエンダ」から生まれている。彼はメキシコの鮮やかな色彩に満たされた優れた現代住宅を設計しているが，故郷の町からメキシコ・シティに移ってきた友人の画家，チューチョ・レイエスは，建物に明るい色彩を使うように彼に勧めていた。もう一人の親友であるポーランド生まれの彫刻家マティアス・ゲーリッツは，この頃にメキシコに移り住み，バラガンと共にメキシコ・シティの都市のシンボルである「サテライト・タワー」をデザインした。バラガンはプリッカー賞を受賞している。

この時代のもう一人の独創的なメキシコ人建築家はマヌエル・パラ（1911-97年）で，彼はサン・カルロス美術学院で建築の訓練を受けた後すぐに，都心の取り壊された住宅から得た古い材料のリサイクルを始め，これらの材料を，彼がサン・アンヘルとコヨアカンの郊外にデザインした2つの新しい住宅に用いた。2つの村は，副王統治時代にスペイン人が別荘として利用していた場所で，そこでの寛いだ時間を楽しむために素晴らしい果樹園を育てていたことだろう。パラは，この特別な場所に独特な空間をつくりだすため，その優れた創造性を駆使して100軒以上の住宅を建設した。それは，訪れる者の目に思いがけないものとして映り，安価で，スペイン人の好みを連想させ，しかもこの地区が都市のイメージを回復するのに役立った。

アカデミックな分野について言えば，『建築の理論』という著作によって強い影響を与えた建築家，ホセ・ビジャグラン・ガルシア（1901-82年）がいる。彼の比類のないデザイン・コンセプトから生まれた建物は，現在でも訪れることができる。

50年代の初めには，メキシコ・シティは目覚ましい建築ブームの舞台となる。その例として，アウグスト・アルバレスによって設計された「ラテンアメリカ・タワー」と「メキシコ・シティ国際空港」があげられよう。彼は合理主義の建築家で，イベロ・アメリカン大学の初代の建築学部長であり，その他数多くの優れた建物で知られる。「メキシコ国立自治大学」のキャンパスは，1951年に200人以上の建築家が参加して建設され，その建築群は最近，UNESCOの世界遺産として登録された。この大学のオープン・スペースの手がかりは明らかに，プレ・ヒスパニック建築から引き出されている。

60年代にペドロ・ラミレス・バスケスとホルヘ・カンプサーノによって設計された「国立人類学博物館」もまた歴史的影響を受けている建築の良い例である。また，1968年にメキシコで開催されたオリンピック大会当時に建てられた名作「カミノ・レアル・ホテル」が，リカルド・レゴレッタの構想により，デザイン・プロセスのコンサルタントとしてマティアス・ゲーリッツ，ルイス・バラガン，チューチョ・レイエスの手を借りて建設された。レゴレッタは多年にわたってホセ・ビジャグラン・ガルシアと共に仕事をし，彼を常に際立った存在にしてきた原則と勇気をビジャグランから学んだ。

最近の数十年の間に，メキシコ・シティの人口は1960年の400万から，今日の

◁▷ *Mexico City's International Airport (left) and Latinamerica Tower, 1956 (right) by Augusto Alvarez*
◁▷ アウグスト・アルバレス設計のメキシコ・シティ国際空港（左）とラテンアメリカ・タワー，1956年（右）

Museum of Anthropology, 1964 by Pedro R. Vazquez and Jorge Campuzano
ペドロ・R・バスケスとホルヘ・カンプザーノ設計の国立人類学博物館（1964年）

chitecture with historical influence. A master piece was built at the time of the Olympic Games held in Mexico in 1968, the 'Camino Real Hotel', conceived by Ricardo Legorreta, and whose consultants in the designing process were Mathias Goeritz, Luis Barragán and Chucho Reyes. Legorreta worked for many years with Jose Villagran Garcia, from whom he learned the discipline and courage that have distinguished him all along.

During the last decades Mexico City has grown tremendously from 4 millions in 1960 to nearly 20 millions in our days. Some very large projects have been put up by several architects, but there are two mature Mexican architects, world wide known, that deserve to be mentioned, both awarded with the Gold Medal from the Union of International Architects: Teodoro Gonzalez de Leon and the above mentioned Ricardo Legorreta. The two have worked in a large variety of buildings: offices, museums, auditoriums, residences, and master plans for urban areas, libraries, universities, and different culture spaces. The impact of Pre-hispanic and Colonial architecture in Gonzalez de Leon (1926-) and Legorreta (1931-) is more than obvious.

There is a great amount of talent among young architects throughout the country at the current time. Most of them are participating in competitions at national and international levels, reconverting cities with new approaches where digital architecture, technology and new materials are considered in the design of innovative structures and sustainable spaces for our present urban life.

Mexico is well known for its long tradition of good architecture, and luckily enough it seems that the new generations are enlarging the scope of this artistic gift.

2,000万人近くへと飛躍的に増加した。何人もの建築家の手によっていくつかの非常に大規模なプロジェクトが進められてきたが，その中でも世界中によく知られ，共に国際建築家連合（UIA）からのゴールド・メダルを授与された2人の円熟したメキシコ人建築家の名を上げるのが適切だろう——テオドロ・ゴンサレス・デ・レオン（1926年〜）と上述したリカルド・レゴレッタ（1931年〜）である。二人は広範な種類の建物に携わってきた。オフィス，美術館，オーディトリアム，住宅，都市の全体計画，図書館，大学，様々な文化施設。プレ・ヒスパニックとコロニアル建築の影響は二人の作品に明白に現れている。

現在，国の至る所で才能豊かな若い建築家が活躍している。彼らのほとんどは国際的なあるいは国家的な設計競技に参加し，デジタル・アーキテクチャー，テクノロジー，新素材など，現代の都市生活のための革新的な構造と，持続可能なスペース・デザインのなかで検討されている新たな手法によって都市の再改造に従っている。

メキシコは優れた建築の長い伝統ゆえによく知られ，幸いなことに，新しい世代はこの芸術的な贈り物の及ぶ範囲をさらに広げているように思われる。

Bernardo Gomez-Pimienta
Enrique Norten

Salas-Basanni House

Valle de Bravo, Mexico, 2001 (renovation)

Entrance: view from patio　エントランス：パティオより見る

Entrance on left: view toward bedroom wing　左にエントランス：正面は寝室棟

Patio: renovation area on left corner パティオ：左側コーナーが改造したエリア

Northwest elevation 北西面

Patio　パティオ

Hacienda

The Spanish immigrants settled in the new continent built up a vast fortune in 16th century from mining silver utilizing aboriginal people as the labor force. However, the silver mining business gradually declined, and those mine owners and landowners shifted their work to the agriculture by forming plantations. Those plantations were called 'Hacienda', and a large scale one consisting of the mansion of the landowner, the houses of the workers, and a church formed a community by itself. The residential building of the wealthy class was a new style based on the traditional European building style brought from Spain with the coloration by the native culture of the Mexican aboriginal people, while the liberal and open climate and character backed up to produce various variants of the new style.

Today those mansions are often diverted to be used as hotels, but the example introduced here was partially renovated as a modern residence by an individual owner.

〈アシエンダ〉

新大陸に入植し，16世紀，銀を発掘したスペイン人は先住民族を労働力として莫大な富を得たが，その後銀鉱業が衰退していくにしたがって，鉱山主や地主は農業にシフトし，大農園（荘園）を形成する。これをアシエンダと呼び，規模の大きなものは，荘園主の住宅や従業員の住居，教会なども含んだ一つのコミュニティを成していた。当時の富裕層の住まいは，スペインから持ち込んだヨーロッパの伝統建築を骨格とし，メキシコの先住民の土着文化によって彩られた新しいスタイルによるもので，様々なバリエーションがおおらかな風土と気風のバックアップを得て作られた。

現在ではホテルに転用されているものが多いが，ここで紹介するのは，個人により一部を現代の住宅として改装したものである。

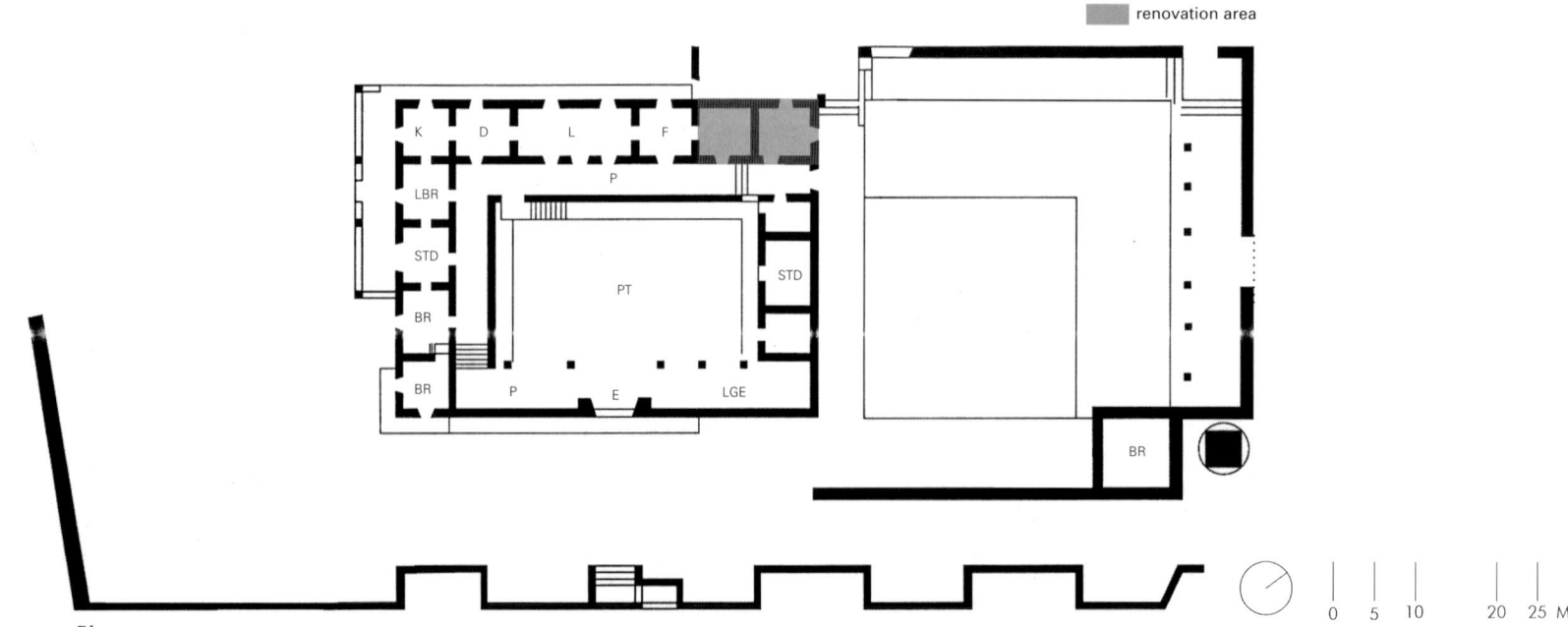

Plan

XVIII century Hacienda located in a hill with view to the lake of Valle de Bravo. The property was dedicated to the agave sowing and its production was destined to the traditional textiles elaboration and a part of, to distillates like the Pulque. Left at the beginning of century XX, the site was falling in deterioration and by a time it served like stable of cows; this use did that it underwent some changes in his form, debilitating the general structure. The acquisition of the property at the beginning of 2000, promoted a plan of general restoration that included reforest of the total plot, with more than 3,000 endemic trees; on the other hand the architectonic project proposed to remove the old wood beams by new of equal dimension and copying the original constructive system. The roofing tiles that were in good conditions were reused to cover the new structure. The walls of adobe and the floors were restored and reinforced. The new area is built in a collapsed area of the property and, by request of the clients, 6 rooms with independent bath were constructed. The addition gives continuity to the heights and proportions of the original construction; giving a contemporary lecture of a traditional house.

Timber work of Hacienda made in XVIII century　18世紀につくられたアシエンダの木組み

18世紀の大農園ハシエンダは，バイエ・デ・ブラボ湖を望む丘に位置していた。この地所では専らリュウゼツランを栽培し，その産物は，手の込んだ伝統的な繊維製品になったり，一部は蒸留されてプルケといった酒になっていた。20世紀初頭になって，この敷地は荒廃していき，時と共に，牛小屋のような使われ方をされた。この用途によって，そのフォルムはいくぶん変形し，構造全体が弱っていった。この地所は2000年初めに入手され，3,000本以上の固有種の木々による敷地全域の森林再生を含む，全面的な修復計画が提唱された。また，一方では，木製の古い梁を，同寸法かつオリジナルの建設方法で複製した新しいものに取り換えるという，建築プロジェクトが提案された。状態の良かった屋根瓦は，新しい構造体を覆うために再利用された。日干し煉瓦の壁と床は，修復され，補強された。新しい空間は，農園の崩壊したエリアに建てられ，また，施主の要望によって，それぞれに浴室のある6室が建築された。この増築部分は，オリジナルの建築の高さとプロポーションを保っている。それは，この増築部分自体が，現代における伝統的な住宅についての講義を行っているようなものである。

Masonry work　石積み

△▽*Patio* パティオ

Portico: clay wall and timber structure for roof　回廊：土壁と木造の小屋組△▽

Portico 回廊

Portico 回廊

Entrance to lounge ラウンジへの入口

Lounge ラウンジ

Living room 居間

Dining room 食堂

23

Renovation area

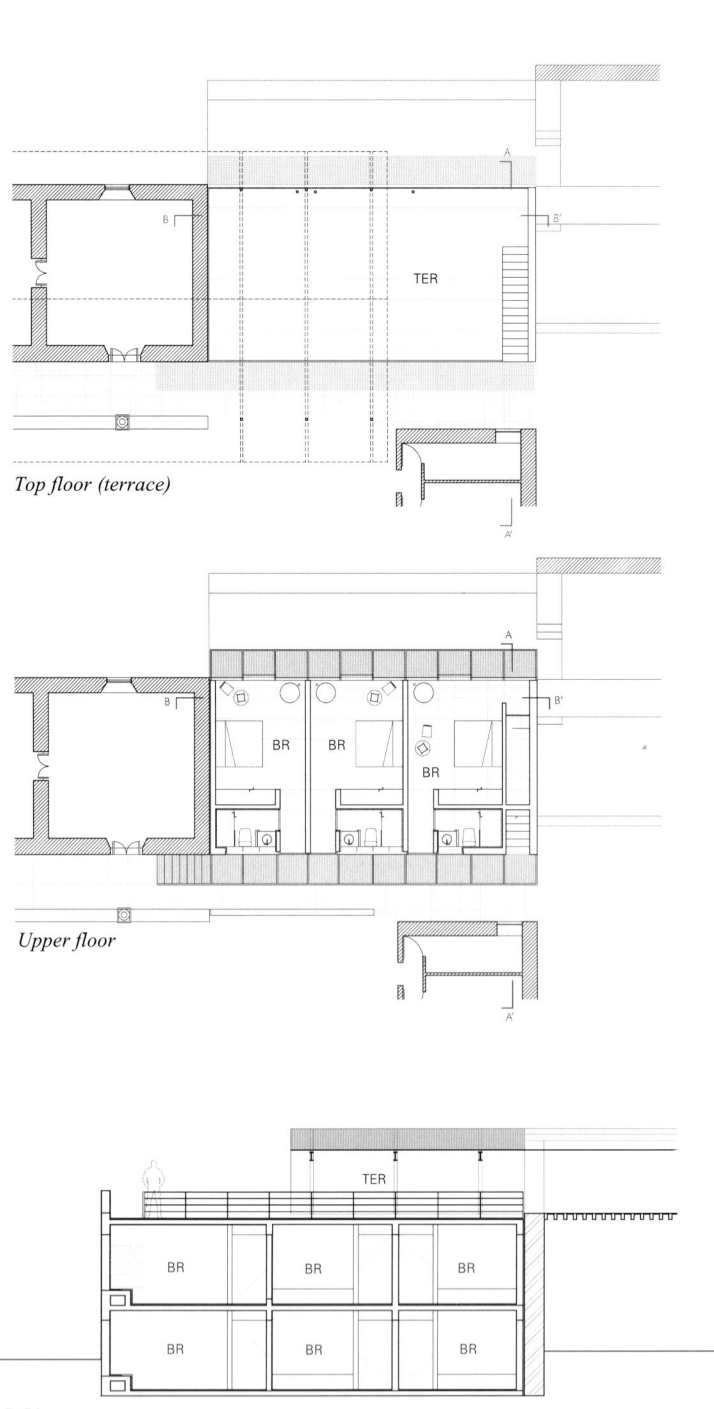

Top floor (terrace)

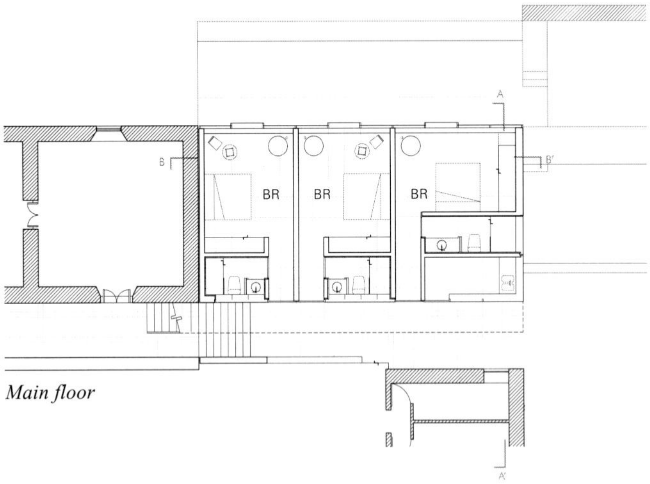

Main floor

Upper floor

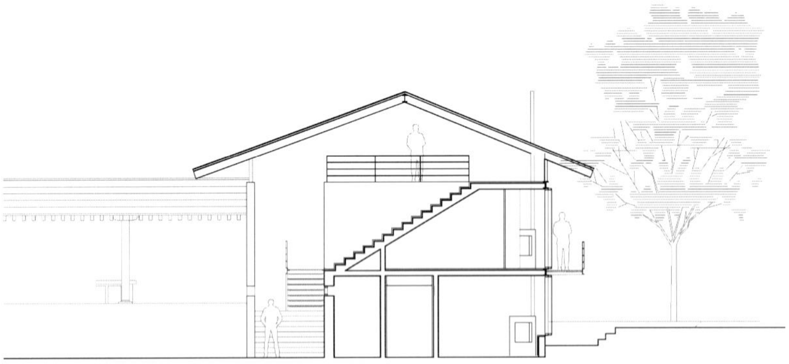

Section A-A'

Section B-B'

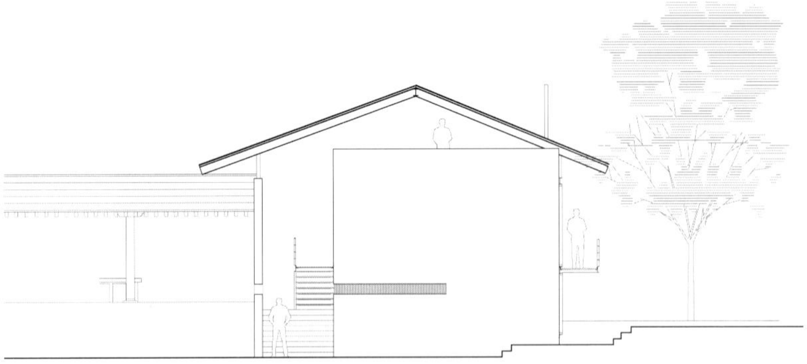

Northeast elevation

Northwest elevation

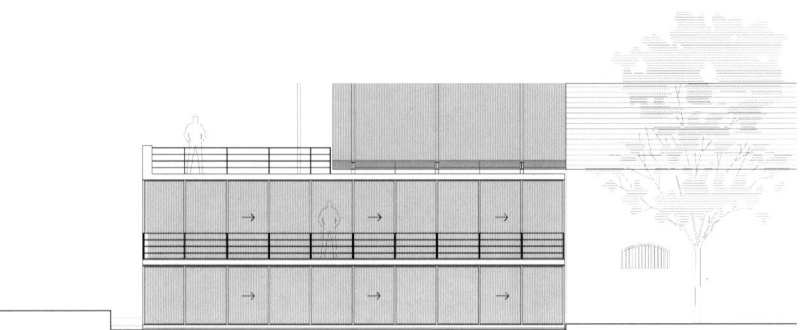

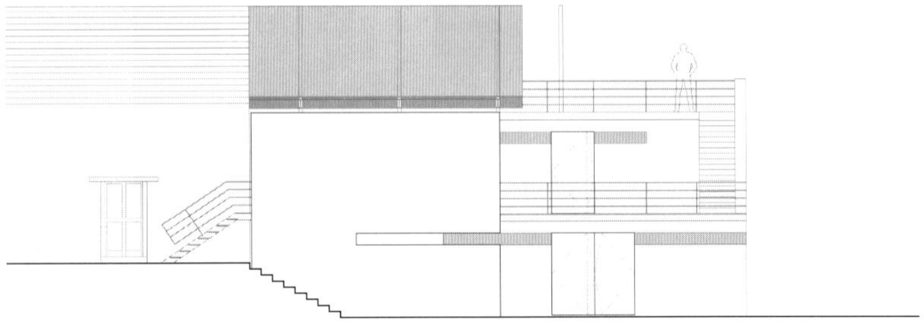

Southeast elevation

Southeast elevation (view from passage)

0 1 2.5 5 10 M

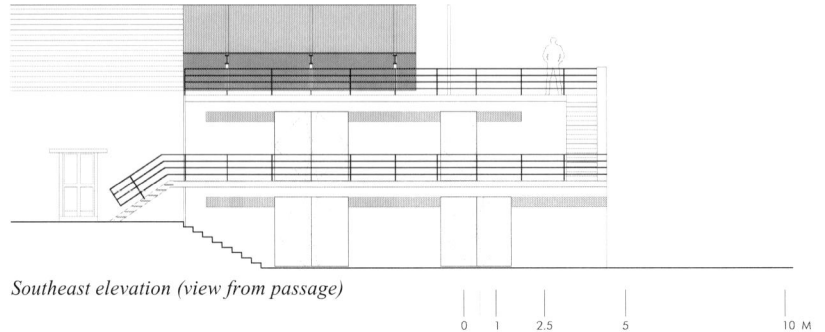

View from northwest: renovation area on left　北西より見る：左は改造したエリア

Pool and bedroom wing　プールと離れの寝室棟

Renovation area: covered passage 改造エリア：通路

Passage connecting between renovation area and existing area
改造エリアと既存エリアを繋ぐ通路

View from patio of renovation area パティオより改造エリアを見る

Passage: view toward existing area 通路：既存エリア方向を見る

Renovation area: view from northwest　改造エリア：北西より見る

△▷*Renovation area: bedroom*　改造エリア：寝室

Renovation area: bedrooms　改造エリア：寝室△▽

Jose Luis Cortes Cortes House

Mexico City, Mexico, 1988– (renovation)

I arrived in Mexico City to live in the historic neighborhood of San Angel, recognized as a colonial village of the sixteenth century, where the Spaniards would spend weekends and holidays in homes surrounded by orchards and farmland.

Being a neighborhood of great historical and cultural context, where famous writers like Octavio Paz and Carlos Fuentes to name a few, as well as philosophers and artists have lived and whose narrow cobblestone streets give it a very particular poetic character, I was instantly captivated by it. During the eighteenth century this was the site of the Goicochea "Hacienda", of which only the manor house remains, now known as "Hacienda" San Ángel Inn.

During the first half of the twentieth century, the painters Diego Rivera and Frida Kahlo both built their studios across the street, designed by Juan O'Gorman. The manor house of the old "hacienda" was used from 1955 to 1960 as the first school of architecture of the Iberoamerican University, of which I am currently the Dean. It was later converted into a restaurant. The house I renovated for myself and turned into my home, is in the block facing this historic site.

Red, ochre and yellow mixed with warm materials and the interplay of the four elements (sun, water, air an earth) that converse as they intertwine in and out of balconies and terraces, stopping to listen to the murmur of water, comforted in the lukewarm natural light that enters through open doors and windows, or taking pleasure in the embers of the enchanting fireplaces of the living room, bedroom or the porch.

My home is always open to greet friends, without whom I never would have conceived or enjoyed this house as it stands now. The main purpose of the renovation has been to create an oasis in the midst of the hustle and bustle of the hectic rhythm of one of the largest cities in the world.

As an architect, it is a big challenge to design one's own space for it entails a deep conversation with one's inner being. The initial confrontation generates a reflective exercise in search of the essence, in order to honestly define what one wants, what one needs, what one desires for a house that will be lived in for many years.

I bought this house blindfolded, mainly because it was across the street where I had been living for thirteen years, near my friends. My father noticed a sign for sale in 1988, in an old tenement house, that I had never even paid attention to because of its deteriorated condition. The site had an interesting shape in the form of an "L", with access from two streets, with great architectural potential.

It also had an interesting social story. This had been the home of a big low-income family, a father with three daughters and his wife of a second marriage and eight children from the previous marriage, all married with their own children. This results in a house of many rooms built in a megastructure. The challenge was how to optimize the use of this compartmentalized space.

The neighborhood was already familiar to me, fact which was fundamental to me. Living in a big metropolis does not weigh on my soul, because I live in an area where I know the people, where I have my own space, and perhaps this is what gives quality of life to my existence.

Following the footsteps of the Mexican architect Manuel Parra, I reused many of the materials from old demolished buildings. Providing continuity to the context of the winding cobblestone streets of San Ángel, I used traditional historic materials such as brownstone, wood, wrought iron on the façade, considering them to be warm materials of local artisans' workshops.

During the course of defining the different spaces, many friends of mine participated, generously giving ideas (Architects Manuel Parra, Carlos San Martin, and Jacques Vermonden among others). My house is really a reflection of my life, a shared experience with the people that are close to me. This house could not have been conceived with a single, predetermined idea, but rather with shared discussions, establishing criteria, accepting the most valuable opinions, exploring and refining them.

I like people to come to my house. I am not a loner, there is always someone dropping in for breakfast, lunch or dinner. Often, there will be reunions to dis-

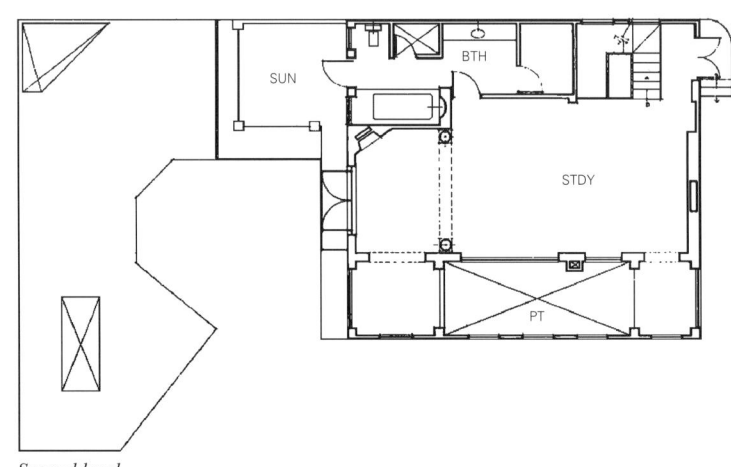

Second level

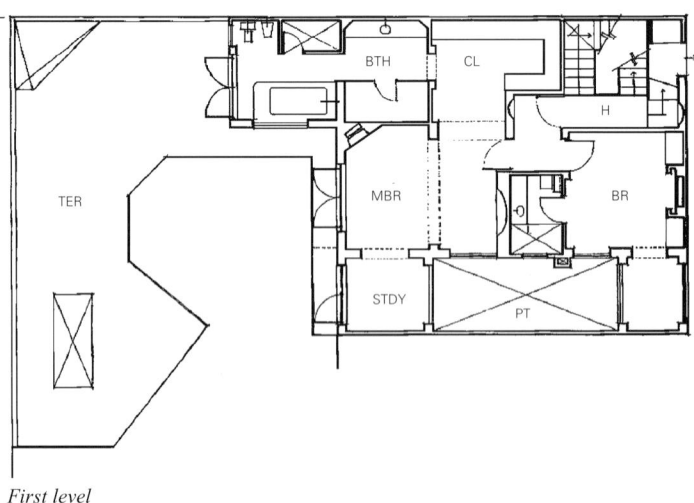

First level

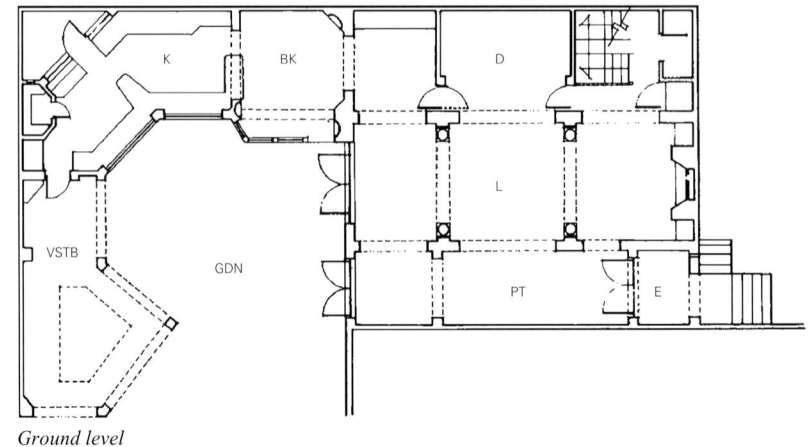

Ground level

cuss literary or professional themes. Nothing is rigid, the ambience changes from day to day. What is in one place one day may be in another the next.

From the very moment you enter the house, you are received by a small brownstone fountain at the entrance with its musical murmur of trickling water, permeating a sense of tranquility. One crosses an exterior patio to enter into an indoor patio bathed in sunlight coming from a very high rooftop dome. This interior triple height patio becomes the integrating element of the house. From here we can enter a very large and welcoming living room, from which we can exit onto a wide terrace which can be intensely "lived-in" at any hour of the day, during any season, thanks to a cozy outdoor fireplace. From this terrace one can view a small pond that immediately becomes the subject of contemplation.

The private quarters are on the second floor and the library is on the third, receiving light all day long from the south. This library is covered by a catalan vault. Coming out onto the terrace, one crosses over to the guest suites, often occupied by visitors from all over the world.

The finishes are simple and modest. Materials that have been given a second chance to play an important role define the personality of this house.

Most of the floors are covered with second hand oak staves, part of the roof was made of slate and beams to strengthen the original structure, shipped from Puebla from demolition sites.

I have been living in this house for 20 years and it has been my greatest pleasure, as well as a challenge, with respect to the process of transformation it has gone through to develop the spaces in relation to the light and the urban context. Architecture is a particular expression. Architects with their buildings are always exposed to criticism. Building one's own home is always a more critical and vulnerable position. This situation is short-lived, though, because the most important thing about designing your own home is that it allows you to consolidate yourself and therefore say "This is who I am".

私がメキシコ・シティにやってきたのは，歴史地区であるサン・アンヘルに住むためであった。ここは16世紀のコロニアルの村として知られ，かつてスペイン人が週末や休暇を，果樹園や農地に囲まれた家で過ごした場所である。

ほんの少数の名をあげても，オクタヴィオ・パスやカルロス・フエンテスなど，著名な作家や哲学者，芸術家が住み，丸石が敷き詰められた細い道が非常に独特な詩的雰囲気を醸し出している，歴史的にも文化的にも重要なコンテクストを持つこの地区に，私はすぐさま虜になった。18世紀，ここはゴイコチェア“アシエンダ”の敷地であった所で，今は，農場時代のマナー・ハウスだけが残り，“アシエンダ”サン・アンヘル・インとして知られる。

20世紀前半に，画家のディエゴ・リベラとフリーダ・カーロがそれぞれのスタジオをホアン・オゴルマンの設計で道の向かい側に建てている。マナー・ハウスは1955年から1960年まで，現在，私が学部長をしているイベロ・アメリカン大学の最初の建築学部として使われていた。後にそれはレストランに改造された。自分自身のために改造し，自宅へと転換させた家は，この歴史的な敷地に面している。

暖かみのある材料と混ぜ合わされた赤，オークル，黄色，そして４つの自然要素（太陽，水，空気，土）が互いに交錯し，バルコニーやテラスの内外で絡み合いながら対話を交わす。水のせせらぎに耳を澄ますために立ち止まり，開け放たれた扉や窓を通って射し込む自然光のぬくもりのなかで安らぎ，あるいは居間や寝室やポーチの魅惑的な暖炉の残り火を楽しむ。

私の家はいつも友達を迎えるために開かれ，今そうであるように，この家を感じ，楽しまなかった人はかつて誰もいない。改造の主な目的は，世界でも最大の都市の一つの熱狂的なリズムを持つ賑わいのなかにオアシスをつくることであった。

建築家として，自分の内的存在との深い会話を引き出すために，自分自身の空間を設計することは大きな挑戦である。最初に直面するのは，長い年月に渡り住むことになる家に対して，自分が欲すること，自分が必要とするもの，自分が願うことをいつわりなく見極めるために，本質を探し求める深い思索を試みることである。

私はこの家を，友達の家の近くにあり，13年間住んできた道の向かい側にあるというのを主な理由に，むこうみずに購入した。父は1988年に，古い共同住宅が売りに出される兆しに気づいていたが，私はその建物があまりに劣化していたために注意さえ払ったことがなかった。敷地は“L”型の面白い形をしていて２つの道路からアクセスでき，建築的には大きな可能性を持っていた。

この家にはまた興味深い，社会的背景があった。これは，３人の娘のいる父親，２度目の妻とその８人の連れ子たち，そのすべてが結婚していて子供がいるという低所得者層の大家族の家であった。この結果，メガストラクチャーのなかに組み込まれた，数多くの部屋を持つ家が生まれた。いかにして，この区分された空間をできるだけ効果的に活用するかが挑戦となった。

この地域は私にはすでに馴染みのある場所であり，事実，私の根底をかたちづくるものとなっていた。大都市に住むことは私の魂にとっては重要なことではない。というのは，自分の知っている人々がいて，自分自身の空間を持つ地域に住んでいるからであり，多分これが，私の存在に生活の質を与えてくれているものなのだ。

メキシコの建築家，マヌエル・パラの足跡に従って，取り壊された古い建物から出た材料の多くを再利用した。サン・アンヘルの丸石の敷かれた曲がりくねる道のコンテクストとの連続性を提供しながら，褐色砂岩，木，鍛鉄のような伝統的，歴史的な材料を，地元のアルチザンの仕事場に特有の暖かい材料となるように考えつつファサードに用いた。

様々なスペースを決めて行く間，数多くの友人（なかでも，建築家のマヌエル・パラ，カルロス・サン・マルティン，ジャック・ベルモンデン）が参加し，惜しみなくアイディアを与えてくれた。この家はまさに私の生活，私に近い人々との共有体験を反映させたものである。それは，単一の，あらかじめ決められたアイディアによって考えられたものではなく，最も価値のある意見を受け入れ，それらを探求し，洗練させ，規準を確立する，共有された議論から生まれている。

私は，人々が家を訪ねてくるのが好きである。私は孤独を好むタイプではないので，いつも誰かが朝食や，ランチあるいは夕飯にぶらりとやってくる。それは，しばしば，文学や専門的なテーマを論じる懇親会となる。固定されたものはひとつもなく，雰囲気は日々変わる。ある日，ある場所にあったものは，次には別の場所になっているかもしれない。

家に入るまさにその瞬間から，エントランスに置かれた，褐色砂岩の小さな噴水と，静けさを浸透させているその少しずつ落ちる水のさらさらという音楽的な調べに迎えられる。戸外のパティオを横切り，ドーム屋根の非常に高い頂きから注ぐ陽射しに満たされた屋内パティオに入る。この３層の高さを持つ屋内パティオはこの家を統合する要素となる。ここから，とても広く，人を歓待してくれる居間に入ることができる。居間からは，気持ちのよい野外の暖炉のおかげで，どの季節にも，１日のどの時間でも，心から“住みつき”たくなるゆったりとしたテラスに出られる。このテラスからは，すぐさま瞑想の対象となってしまう，小さな池が見える。

私的な領域は２階にあり，南からの陽射しを一日中受ける３階にはライブラリーがある。ライブラリーはカタロニア・ヴォールトで覆われている。テラスへ出て，ゲスト・スイートへ横切って行く。ここにはたいてい世界中からの客が宿泊している。

仕上げはシンプルで控えめなものにしている。材料には，この家の個性を規定する重要な役割を演じる２番目のチャンスが与えられている。

床の大半は，中古のカシの樽板を張り詰め，屋根の一部は，取り壊しの現場であるプエブラから搬送したオリジナルの構造体を強化するためのスレートと梁で構成されている。

私はこの家に，光と都市のコンテクストと関わるように空間を展開させてきたその変貌のプロセスを大切にしながら20年間住んできたが，それは大きな喜びであり，挑戦であり続けてきた。建築は個別的な表現である。設計したその建物と共に建築家は常に批判に晒される。その自邸の建設となれば常に，さらに多くの批判や攻撃をうけやすい立場を導く。しかし，この状況は束の間のことに過ぎない。自邸を設計する上で最も重要な点は，自分自身を整理し固めさせてくれることにあり，それゆえに，“これが私です”と言わせてくれるのだ。

Pass to garden 中庭へ続く通路

View from street 道路より見る

△▷ *Garden* 中庭

Living room　居間△▽

Upward view of patio　パティオ見上げ

Fireplace of living room　居間の暖炉

Approach: staircase to entrance　アプローチ：入口へ続く階段

Staircase: view toward entrance　階段室：入口を見る

Staircase: view from entrance　階段室：入口より見る

Patio　パティオ

Living room: view toward fireplace　居間：暖炉方向を見る

View toward patio from living room　居間よりパティオを見る

Study on second floor: vaulted ceiling made of brick 　3階書斎：煉瓦造のヴォールト天井

Study on second floor: looking upper part of patio through openings 　3階書斎：開口部を通してパティオ上部を見る

'Revolution and Evolution'
The Rise of the Modern House in Mexico
Alejandro Aptilon

革命と変遷—
メキシコにおける近代住宅の興隆
アレハンドロ・アプティロン

Therein lies the lesson that modern Mexico can provide us. It takes the forms of the European machinist civilization and adapts them to its own spirit.
Antonin Artaud, Mexico, 1936[1]

The dictum 'Architecture ou révolution' greatly influenced both European thought and Mexican architectural practice. While in Europe theoretical works advised that architecture was the way to avoid social uprising, ironically in Mexico it was the revolution of 1910 that brought about authentic change in building practice, turning it within a few years toward a deeply functionalist approach. This unique process is clearly reflected in the evolution of single-family dwelling projects during the first half of the century; tracing the transformation of the house is essential in order to understand the evolving character of Mexican modern architecture. As we will see, soon after the Spartan functionalist style of building was introduced in Mexico, it became so dogmatic there that its spell lasted only a couple of decades before a revisionist impulse prevailed among leading architects, several of whom had been founders of the original functionalist movement, prompting them to return to a traditional approach.

In 1920, the end of the decade-long armed struggle of the first revolution of the century brought great optimism and expectation for real change among the Mexican population, along with the necessity for a new order. The recently installed government of President Álvaro Obregón (1920-24) sought a national identity that would replace the prevailing and deeply rooted French influence that had characterized the culture of the overthrown Porfirian dictatorship era. Progressive intellectual and artistic circles expressed great enthusiasm for renewal, as they hoped to minimize the consciousness of postwar hardships.

By 1922, José Vasconcelos, head of the newly created Secretaría de Educación Pública (Ministry of Culture), had carried out a messianic educational and cultural crusade whose impact was to last for decades to come. Urged by the immediate need of a new infrastructure, Vasconcelos also created the Departamento de Construcción de la Secretaría de Educación Pública, of which the architect José Villagrán (1901-82) was a member. Villagrán built for the Departamento some of the most progressive building complexes of that time. A graduate of the Escuela Nacional de Bellas Artes in a period of imminent change during the 1920's, Villagrán was deeply influenced by French nineteenth-century theory. His buildings erected during that decade exemplified the fulfillment of post-revolutionary needs through architecture. His designs were based above all on a meticulous analysis of the program: 'The forms should be conceived as a result rather than a starting point', he said, devoid of any ornamentation and executed with as simply as possible for maximum functionality. His work thus became the precursor of the functionalist movement.

近代メキシコが我々に与えることのできる教訓がそこにある。ヨーロッパの機械文明のかたちを取り入れ，それらを自身の精神に適合すること。
アントナン・アルトー，メキシコ，1936[1]

「建築か革命か」という言明は，ヨーロッパの思考とメキシコの建築的実践の双方に大きな影響を与えた。ヨーロッパでは，建築理論が，建築は社会的反乱を避ける方法であると提言したが，皮肉なことにメキシコでは，建設の現場に確実な変化をもたらし，わずか数年のうちに徹底した機能主義へと向かわせたのが1910年の革命だった。この独特な展開は，20世紀前半の50年間における一戸建て住宅の展開に明快に反映されている。住宅の変遷を辿ることは，メキシコの近代建築の発展が帯びている特徴を理解するために不可欠である。予測されるように，建物の厳格な機能主義スタイルがメキシコに導入されると間もなく，それは非常に教条的なものになり，機能主義の魅力が保たれたのは，指導的建築家の間にそれを修正しようという衝動が広がる前の数十年間にすぎなかった。伝統的な方法への回帰を押し進めた指導的建築家の幾人かは，機能主義運動の創始者でもあったのである。

1920年，20世紀の最初の革命となった10年にわたる武力抗争の終結は，メキシコ大衆の間に，新しい秩序と共に現実の変化に対する大きな楽観と期待をもたらした。新たに就任したアルバロ・オブレゴン大統領政権（1920-24年）は，打倒されたポルフィリオ独裁時代の特徴的な文化であり，その時代を席巻し，そこに深く根ざしていたフランスの影響に代わり得る国家のアイデンティティを探し求めた。進歩的な知識人や芸術家のサークルは戦後の困難に対する意識を最小限に抑えることを願いながら，再生への強い熱意を表明した。

1922年，新設された文部省の長官，ホセ・バスコンセロスは，来たるべき数十年間にわたって影響を及ぼすことになる救世主的な教育，文化改革運動を行った。新しい社会を支える基本的施設の差し迫った必要にせきたてられて，バスコンセロスはまた文部省内に建設局を設立し，建築家のホセ・ビジャグラン（1901-82年）をその一員とした。ビジャグランはここで，当時として最も進歩的な建築コンプレックスのいくつかを建設した。1920年代の一触即発の時代に国立芸術大学を卒業したビジャグランは，フランス19世紀の理論に深く影響されていた。建設局にあった10年間に建てられた彼の建物は，建築を通して革命後の必要を満たす範例となった。彼のデザインは何よりもプログラムの緻密な分析に基づいている。「形態は出発点ではなく結果として考えるべきである」と彼は述べ，機能性を最大限に実現するために，いかなる装飾も避け，可能な限りシンプルにつくりあげた。彼の作品はこうして，機能主義運動の先駆となった。

新しい建築に対する願望については，20世紀初頭の10年間，伝統的なものと，輸入された装飾主義の両方が並行する転換期の間，既に論争が行われてきた。ビジャグランでさえその渦中に居たのだが，1922年から1927年にかけて，強い国粋

A desire for a new architecture was already being debated in the first decade of the twentieth century, during a parallel transition period of both traditional and imported ornamentation in which even Villagrán played a role; and from 1922 to 1927, a strong nationalist movement arose. Since 1913 the architects Federico Mariscal and Jesús T. Acevedo had lectured about the need to return to the roots of Mexican culture, which they related to the three Viceroyal centuries, during which, they claimed, the Mexican race was consolidated out of Spanish and local native blood.[2] Traditionalist and nationalist architecture was also influenced by revolution-inspired songs and literary genres, and also ironically by the fashionable 'Hollywood Spanish' architectural style of the time.[3]

The Ermita-Isabel complex on Avenida Revolución built between 1928 and 1932 by Juan Segura (1898-1989) illustrates the desire at that time to enclose the latest amenities and services within a traditional-looking composition. A visual and functional hybrid, and the first New-York-style multipurpose complex in Mexico, it includes commercial, housing and entertaining facilities in two architectural bodies: the 'Edificio Ermita' (1930-32), an eight-story apartment structure that includes a large movie theater, in a triangular plan reminiscent of Daniel Burnham's 'Flatiron Building', and the four-story 'Edificio Isabel compound' (1928-29), whose lower profile allowed it to blend with the existing urban fabric. The Isabel is composed of two groups of townhouses, each set along a courtyard-like interior street, with commercial facilities on the outside periphery. The housing development was targeted to middle-class refugees of the revolution who had moved to the city, and it has an urban-provincial crossbreed style that combines Art Deco and traditional Mexican ornamentation. Segura's complex serves as an example of this early transition period also in that its advanced structure combines steel with reinforced concrete, materials that were being widely used in Mexico by the time of its completion.

Mexican architects and engineers first acknowledged the concept of modernity in architecture through the influence of foreign works, which appeared in both local and imported publications, as well as through the generalized use of concrete; its widespread practice was triggered, however, by the urgent needs and profound idealism inherited from the 1910 revolution. The magazines *Cemento* and *Tolteca*, created in1925 and 1929 respectively by an association of cement factories, advocated the use of concrete, and since 1924 the architecture section of the local newspaper *Excelsior* had also published works by Hans Poelzig, Robert Mallet-Stevens, Erich Mendelsohn, Joseph Hoffman, Le Corbusier, and others. Concrete became the immediate solution for rapid, low-budget construction favored by engineers.[4] Then, during the decade-long revolution, economic constraints led to the adoption of poorly finished and exposed construction materials, which eventually became an acquired and accepted taste for exterior finishes. Reinforced concrete eventually came to

主義運動が起こる。1913年以来，建築家フェデリコ・マリスカルとヘスス・T・アセベドは，メキシコ文化のルーツに回帰する必要について講演していた。彼らは副王統治の続いた3つの世紀に関係づけ，その間，メキシコ民族は，スペイン人と先住民族の血筋の中に統合されたと主張した。[2] 伝統主義者と国家主義者の建築は革命に鼓舞された歌や文学のジャンルにも影響され，そしてまた皮肉なことに，当時のファッショナブルな「ハリウッド・スパニッシュ」の建築様式にも影響されていた。[3]

1928年から1932年にかけて建てられた，ホアン・セグラ（1898-1989年）のレフォルマ通りに面した「エルミータ＝イサベル・コンプレックス」は伝統的な外貌を見せる構成のなかに最新のアメニティとサービスを収めるという当時の願望を示している。視覚的なものと機能的なものの混在，メキシコにおける最初のニューヨーク・スタイルの多目的複合建築であるこの建物には商業施設，集合住宅，娯楽施設が2棟の建築に収められている。8階建ての住戸棟「エルミータ・ビル」（1930-32年）には大きな映画館が含まれ，ダニエル・バーナムの「フラットアイアン・ビル」を連想させる三角形プランを持ち，4階建ての「イサベル・ビル・コンパウンド」（1928-29年）は，その低層の輪郭によって既存の町並みに溶け込んでいる。この建物は2組のタウンハウスで構成され，それぞれ中庭のような内部道路に沿い，商業施設が外縁に配置されている。集合住宅は都市に流入してきた革命からの中流の避難民向けに開発されたもので，アール・デコと伝統的なメキシコの装飾を組み合わせた，都市的なものと地方的なものを異種交配させたスタイルを備えている。セグラのコンプレックスはその先進的な構造という点で，また，スティールとその完成当時メキシコで広く使われていた材料である鉄筋コンクリートを組み合わせていることでも，この初期の転換期の代表例としての役割を果たしている。

メキシコの建築家とエンジニアは，建築におけるモダニティの概念を，国内のそして輸入された出版物の両方に掲載された海外の作品の影響を通して，また同時に一般に広がっていたコンクリートの使用を通して，最初に知った。しかし，その実施の広範な普及は，急を要する状況と1910年の革命から受け継がれた深い理想主義によって誘発されたものである。1925年に創刊され，1929年からセメント工業協会に引き継がれた雑誌『セメント』と『トルテカ』はコンクリートの使用を推奨し，1924年からは地方紙の『エスセルシオール』の建築欄もまたハンス・ペルツィヒ，ロベルト・マレ＝ステヴァン，エリッヒ・メンデルゾーン，ヨーゼフ・ホフマン，ル・コルビュジエなどの作品を掲載した。コンクリートは瞬く間にエンジニアの支持を獲得した，迅速で低コストの工法となった。[4] その後，十年にわたる革命の間，経済的圧迫は，貧弱な仕上げと，剥き出しのままの建設材料の採用へと導き，コンクリートは結局，外観の仕上げとして好まれ，受け入れられるものになっていった。鉄筋コンクリートはようやくエンジニアにも建築家にも好まれる材料となり，後には，革命後の理想化された美学へと発展して行

be the preferred material for both engineers and architects, and later developed into an idealized post-revolution aesthetic. Engineers tended to take charge of both design and construction in Mexico for most of the first half of the twentieth century, up to the 1950's.[5] At the same time, architects acted as builders in order to increase their income, while engineers offered design services included as part of their development packages. People often confused architects with engineers, and this confusion grew during the 1920's due to the increasing aesthetic and practical convergence of the two professions. This blending of the two trades illustrates how deeply modernity was being assimilated into Mexican building practice by that time.

The work of Francisco Serrano (1900-82), like that of Juan Segura, illustrates this transition to modernity that was occurring in Mexico. Inspired by his father, a well established civil engineer and developer, Serrano was himself educated and trained as an engineer from 1917 to 1920, and in 1938 he completed his studies in architecture at the Escuela Nacional de Arquitectura. A lifetime teacher who educated an entire generation of architects and engineers, his prolific career included the design and construction of some 138 single-family houses. Typical of the engineering practice of the time, Serrano's early work, prior to his architectural training, is surprisingly 'modern' in its conception and execution. Between 1927 and 1932, he was commissioned by De la Lama and Basurto, owners of the new development of Hipódromo de la Condesa, to build fifty promotional houses. Averaging 180 square meters of built area within 250-square-meter lots, the houses were asymmetrical in plan, built out of reinforced concrete frame and brick bearing walls, though designed in at least three style variants to choose from. This ambivalence of style, which oscillated from Art Deco to pseudo-functionalist to California Colonial, characterized Serrano's career until the early fifties, when he completely adopted the by then well-established modern trend. His stylistic stammering, however, diminished his popularity in the architectural community.

Just as engineers practiced architecture, many architects were ready to push their work to the no-frills limits of engineering. Villagrán taught composition and theory from 1924 to 1935, using as the basis of his lectures nineteenth-century French analytical works such as *Elements et Theorie de L'Architecture* by Julien Guadet. Among the first generation of students influenced by his teachings were Enrique del Moral, Alvaro Aburto, Juan Legarreta, and Juan O'Gorman, who also worked for him. O'Gorman had a reputation among his peers as an enfant terrible with an audacious and daring personality, and his practical career began at an early age. Profoundly influenced by Villagrán and his other teachers, José Antonio Cuevas and Guillermo Zárraga, as well as by the first copies to arrive in Mexico of Le Corbusier's *Vers une Architecture*, O'Gorman, to-

く。20世紀前半の大半，1950年代に至るまで，メキシコでは，エンジニアがデザインと建設の両方を引き受ける傾向があった。[5] 同時に，建築家は収入を増やすために建設業者としての仕事をする一方，エンジニアは彼らの開発パッケージの一部としてデザイン・サービスを提供した。人々はしばしば建築家とエンジニアを混同し，この混同は，1920年代の間，2つの専門職の美学的，実践的相似のために大きくなっていった。2つの職業間でのこうした混合は，当時のメキシコにおいて建築の実践の場にモダニティがいかに深く吸収されていたかを示している。

フランシスコ・セラーノ（1900-82年）の作品は，ホアン・セグラの作品のように，メキシコに起きたこのモダニティへの移行を実証している。成功を収めた土木技師であり開発業者であった父親に影響されて，セラーノ自身は1917年から1920年にかけてエンジニアとしての教育と訓練を受け，1938年，国立建築大学で建築の勉強を終えた。建築家とエンジニアのあらゆる世代を指導し，終生，教師であり続けたその実り多いキャリアには，138戸ほどの独立住宅の設計と建設が含まれる。当時の工学技術の仕事の典型である，建築的な修練を受ける前のセラーノの初期作品は，そのコンセプトと手法において驚くほど「近代的」である。1927年から1932年の間，彼は，イポドロモ・デ・ラ・コンデーサ地区の新たな開発のオーナーであるデ・ラ・ラーマとバスルトから50戸の販売促進のための住宅の建設を依頼された。平均で，250平米の敷地，建築面積180平米の住宅は，鉄筋コンクリートのフレームに煉瓦の耐力壁で建設され，非対称のプランで構成されているが，選ぶとすれば少なくとも3種のパターンが挙げられる。アール・デコから疑似機能主義，カリフォルニア・コロニアルに至る，スタイルのこの曖昧さは，50年代の初期，彼が十分に確立された近代的なトレンドに完全に適応する時まで，セラーノの作品を特徴づけている。しかし，その様式的なためらいは，建築界での彼の評判を傷つけるものとなった。

建築に熟達したエンジニアと同様に，多くの建築家は，彼らの仕事を工学技術の実質本位の限界にまで押し進める準備ができていた。ビジャグランは1924年から1935年にかけて構成と理論を，彼の講義の基盤をジュリアン・ガデの『建築の諸要素と理論』のような19世紀フランスの分析的著作を用いて教えていた。彼の教えに影響を受けた学生の最初の世代には，エンリケ・デル・モラル，アルバロ・アブルト，ホアン・レガレッタ，そして彼の元で働いてもいたホアン・オゴルマンがいる。オゴルマンは，独創性に富む豪放な性格を持つアンファン・テリブルとして仲間うちで評価を得ており，彼の実践的なキャリアは若くして始まった。ビジャグランや他の教師，ホセ・アントニオ・クエバス，ギエルモ・サラーガ，またル・コルビュジエの『建築をめざして』のメキシコに到着した最初の版からの影響を深く受けて，オゴルマンは学生仲間のアルバロ・アブルト，ホアン・レガレッタと共に，彼らがフンショナリスモ（機能主義）と呼ぶ，ル・コルビュジエ自身のそれにも増して，信念において過激な方向に走った。彼らは，建築は何よりも実用的な仕事であり，純粋に機能的であるべきで，いかなる美的質

gether with his school colleagues Álvaro Aburto and Juan Legarreta, developed what they called funcionalismo, a trend more radical in conviction than even that of Le Corbusier himself. They held that architecture was above all a utilitarian trade that was to be purely functional, devoid of any aesthetic quality. Legarreta uttered provocative statements such as 'I don't deal with beauty'; Aburto argued in a 1933 lecture that 'Our architecture has to be as poor, bare and naked as we the Mexican people are'; and O'Gorman referred to his own work as 'technical architecture.'

In 1928, at age 23, O'Gorman put his beliefs into practice with an audacious design for a house for the prominent engineer Ernesto Martinez de Alba, which he subsequently built in the newest and most luxurious residential area of Mexico City, Chapultepec Heights. This house was austere yet lavish in comparison to his later work, and incorporated decorative elements composed in an apparent combination of Corbusian influence and Art Deco arrangement that was employed here and never afterward. Later, within less than a decade, O'Gorman designed and built several hard-core functionalist houses, which enabled him to give greater expression to his extreme views. Commissioned by prominent intellectuals and professionals, these houses gave O'Gorman the perfect opportunity to express a clear typology based on pure function. Elements he employed ranged from floor-to-ceiling glass walls and a sawtooth roof for painting studios to a half-domed astronomical observatory. These houses included that for his father, a retired historian and painter, Cecil O'Gorman (1929), which O'Gorman himself considered the first functionalist house in Mexico; one for astronomer Luis Enrique Erro (1933); and a pair of two attached units for Diego Rivera and Frida Kahlo (1932). All clearly Le Corbusier-inspired, these houses went a step further in their bald functional expression and experimentation. Diego's and Frida's houses expose reticular reinforced concrete slabs complete with clay brick infill and use the elevated water tanks as compositional elements. During the same period, the 1932 competition for the Minimal Worker's House sponsored by the cement company Tolteca, and organized by the Departamento del Distrito Federal—the local authorities—under Zárraga, illustrates the official recognition that modern architecture had attained. Legarreta's entry won the first prize, followed by an ingenious double-height solution by Enrique Yañez.

Both architects and engineers in Mexico came to conceive of construction through a method of simplification that was employed almost as an axiomatic formula. As early as the mid-1920's, intellectual leaders were competing for recognition of their work as modern architecture. In 1926 even Diego Rivera claimed that a design of his was the first modern building in Mexico, because of its lack of ornamentation. By the 1930's modern architecture was well established, mainly in Mexico City.[6] Most of the capital's new buildings were, with more or less aesthetic value,

も回避しなければならないと確信していた。レガレッタは「私は美しさとは取引しない」というような挑発的な宣言を述べ、アブルトは1933年の講義で「我々の建築は、我々メキシコの人民のごとく、貧しく、むきだしの裸であるべきだ」と主張し、オゴルマンは自身の作品を「テクニカル・アーキテクチャー」として言及した。

1928年，23歳のとき，オゴルマンは，彼が継続して建てることになる，メキシコ・シティの最も新しく，最も贅沢な住宅地区であるチャプルテペック・ハイツに建つことになる，著名なエンジニア，エルネスト・マルティネス・デ・アルバ邸のための非常に奇抜なデザインにその信念を注ぎ込んだ。この住宅は，彼の後期の作品と較べると，簡潔ではあるが贅沢で，ここだけで，その後は決して採用することのなかった，ル・コルビュジエ風の影響とアール・デコの翻案の明らかな組み合わせのなかに構成された装飾的なエレメントが取り込まれている。その後，10年を経ずしてオゴルマンは，自身の極端な考え方をより大きく表現した，いくつかの筋金入りの機能主義住宅を設計し，建てている。著名な知識人や専門職のクライアントから依頼されたこれらの住宅は，純粋な機能に基づいた明快なタイポロジーを表現する完璧な機会をオゴルマンに与えた。彼が採用したエレメントには，床から天井まで広がるガラス壁から，鋸屋根の絵画スタジオ，半円ドームの天体観測用望楼などに及ぶ。これらの住宅には，オゴルマン自身がメキシコで最初の機能主義住宅とみなしていた，引退した歴史家であり画家である父親の「セシル・オゴルマンのための住宅」(1929年)をはじめ，「天文学者ルイス・エンリケ・エルロの家」(1933年)，2つの連結ユニットで構成され対になった「ディエゴ・リベラとフリーダ・カーロの家」(1932年)が含まれる。すべてが明らかにル・コルビュジエに触発され，これらの住宅はその大胆な機能的表現と実験のなかでさらに一歩を踏み出している。ディエゴとフリーダのそれぞれの住宅は格子状の鉄筋コンクリート・スラブを露出させ，粘土製の煉瓦を充填して塞ぎ，持ち上げた貯水タンクを構成要素として活用している。同時期に行われた1932年の，セメント会社のトルテカが後援し，サラガの下，地方政府である連邦地区省が計画した最小限労働者住宅の設計競技は，近代建築が獲得した公的な承認を示している。レガレッタの応募案は1等となり，エンリケ・ヤニェスの独創的な2層吹き抜けとなった案がそれに続いた。

メキシコでは，建築家とエンジニアの両者が，ほとんど原則的な公式として採用された単純化の方法を通して建設を考えるようになっていた。早くも1920年代の中期から，知的なリーダーたちは彼らの作品を近代建築として認められることを競っていた。1926年，ディエゴ・リベラでさえ，彼のデザインをその装飾の欠如ゆえにメキシコにおける最初の近代建築であったと主張している。[6] 1930年代ごろまでには，近代建築は主にメキシコ・シティでは十分に確立されていた。首都の新しい建物の大半は，多かれ少なかれ美的価値の点で，その性格において近代的なものであった。『アーキテクチュラル・レヴュー』誌のためにメキシコ特別

Plaza de las Fuentes, El Pedregal Garden (Mexico City, 1948-49) by Luis Barragán
ルイス・バラガンによるペドレガル庭園の広場（メキシコ・シティ，1948-49年）

Animal del Pedregal (El Pedregal Garden, 1950) by Mathias Goeritz
マティアス・ゲーリッツよる彫刻"アニマル・デル・ペドレガル"（ペドレガル庭園，1950年）

modern in nature. Esther Born, a photographer and journalist who worked on a special issue about Mexico for the magazine Architectural Review, was surprised to encounter in 1937 a city of mostly modern construction: 'The quantity of it [modern architecture] comes as a surprise. Such a quantity would be unexpected in any North American City; but...he energy displayed and up-to-the-minute quality are doubly astonishing.'(7)

Though the convergence of architecture and engineering continued during the 1930's apparently some professionals were convinced enough of the difference between the two trades that they paired their practices to complement each other in a rather successful way. The engineer-architect partnership of Francisco Martinez Negrete and Luis Martínez Negrete had established a practice for wealthy clients, and were already designing and building clean-cut modern house and apartment buildings for at least six years before Born arrived in Mexico. The 'Palomino House' (1931), located on Río Tigris street in the new Cuauhtémoc neighborhood, next to Reforma Avenue, was a three-story single-family unit set back on a generous lot, and included a double-height living room, as well as a bathroom for each of the two bedrooms. Horizontal window bands and soft curves strategically placed were used to soften the stark prismatic composition. The white plush style of villa built by the Martínez Negrete team demonstrated the wide acceptance of their approach within the highest social strata, which meant not only that this trend had moved from the economically constrained classes into more exclusive circles, but also that modern style had ultimately become fashionable.

In 1935 Villagrán built his own house at the stylish Colonia Juárez on the opposite side of Reforma Avenue, and here, unlike the Martínez Negrete houses, austere components seem to have been placed with more utilitarian than compositional concerns. This structure clearly expresses Villagrán's rational pragmatism, which gave birth to the functionalist movement. Set on the western portion of the lot in order to achieve maximum southeast sun exposure, the house has windows whose shapes varied according to need. Corner windows, reserved exclusively for the master bedroom, modestly reveal the free façade concept and concrete structure of the house. Curves, which even the pragmatic O'Gorman used in his compositions, are conspicuously absent in this and most of Villagrán's work. In a manner consistent with his function-oriented program, Villagrán exploited the roof surface for different uses: terrace, sunbathing, and laundry. The reinforced concrete frame structure is visible in its interior, as part of the openly-exposed spirit of the house.

Luis Barragán (1902-88) was another figure initially trained as an engineer with a complementary architectural education, and like Serrano, his early work exemplifies the modernity embedded in the spirit of the builder. From 1936 to 1940, Barragán designed and built more than a dozen speculative projects, and he deemed this period his 'commercial

号に携わった写真家でありジャーナリストであるエッサー・ボーンは，1937年に，ほとんどが近代建築で埋まるメキシコ・シティと出会って驚かされた。「その"近代建築"の多さは思いがけないものであった。これほどの数は北アメリカのどの都市にも見られないだろう。しかも……表現されたもののエネルギーと最新の優れた質はそれに倍加する驚きである」(7)

建築と工学技術の一体化は1930年代を通じて続いたが，明らかに幾人かのプロフェッショナルは，2つの職業の違いを十分に得心し，彼らは互いに補完しあうために仕事で組んではるかに成功を収めた。フランシスコ・マルティネス・ネグレテとルイス・マルティネス・ネグレテによるエンジニアと建築家の協同によって富裕なクライアントのための事務所が確立され，ボーンがメキシコに到着する前の，少なくとも6年間に既に紛れも無い近代住宅やアパートメント・ビルディングが設計され，建設されていた。レフォルマ通りに隣接する新しいクワウテモク地区のリオ・ティグリス通りに面する「パロミノ邸」（1931年）は広い敷地にセットバックして建てられた3階建ての独立住宅で，2層吹き抜けの居間と，浴室付きの寝室2つが含まれている。効果的に配置された水平の連続窓と緩やかなカーブが厳しいプリズムのような構成を和らげている。マルティネス・ネグレテのチームにより建てられたヴィラの白く贅沢なスタイルは，上流階級のなかで彼らの手法が広く受け入れられていることを示し，それはこのトレンドが経済的に制約された階級からより上流のサークルに移動したことばかりでなく，モダン・スタイルがついに，流行のものになったことを意味している。

1935年，ビジャグランは，レフォルマ通りの反対側に面した当世風のコロニア・フアレスに自邸を建て，ここではマルティネス・ネグレテの住宅作品とは違い，簡潔な諸要素が構成的配慮よりも実用性を重んじて配置されているように見える。この建物は，機能主義運動を誕生させたビジャグランの合理的実用主義を明快に表現している。南東の陽射しに最大限向けるため敷地の西側の場所に配置された住宅には，必要に応じて様々なかたちの窓がとられている。主寝室のためだけに確保された隅窓は，この家の自由なファサードとコンクリート構造をひかえめに見せている。実用主義者であるオゴルマンでさえ彼の構成の中に用いた曲線は，この建物やビジャグランのほとんどの作品には欠如しているのが目につく。彼の機能指向のプログラムと首尾一貫する方法のなかで，ビジャグランは屋上をテラス，日光浴，ランドリーと異なった使い方に利用している。鉄筋コンクリート造フレーム架構は，この家の包み隠さずオープンにするという精神の一部としてその内部空間から見ることができる。

ルイス・バラガン（1902-88年）は，最初はエンジニアとして訓練され，補完的に建築の教育を受けたもう一人の著名な人物であり，セラーノのように彼の初期の作品はビルダーの精神のなかに近代性が埋め込まれている好例である。1936年から1940年にかけてバラガンは1ダース以上の投機的なプロジェクトを設計し建設しており，彼はこの時期を彼の「コマーシャル・エポック」とみなしていた。こ

Gómez House (1951-52) by Francisco Artigas
フランシスコ・アルティガス設計，ゴメス邸（1951-52年）

epoch.' The third project of this period, his 1936 pair of attached townhouses facing Parque México in Colonia Hipódromo de la Condesa, were built almost ten years after Serrano's first intervention in the same area, which by now was fashionable and highly in demand, hence the desire to achieve maximum density. As stated earlier, modern style was by then a product targeted to the middle and upper middle classes, and the compact nature of the project was probably inspired by contemporary works that Barragán had seen in his earlier travels to Europe and the United States, as 'simplified living' was already the trend of interest in every modern city.[8] In a narrow nine-meter-wide lot Barragán managed to project two three-story dwellings, taking advantage of the protrusion of the northern house to create corner windows in outward and inset variations (later altered to be equal) in order to exploit maximum views towards the park, and to create a larger interior space effect. Here too, the influence of Le Corbusier's versatility is present both in the carefully composed 'free facades' and the use of the top slab as a roof garden. Barragán made use of his early but already refined sensibility to create a dynamic interaction of planes that opens to the sky, a formula he would later use in the polychrome version roof terrace of his own house at Tacubaya in 1947.

Around the same time, Barragán had already ventured into the large-scale development range with his design for the 'Jardines del Pedregal' neighborhood in the south of the capital, paving the way for a new trend of unprecedented experimentation with modernity in Mexico. Francisco Artigas (1916-99), a native of the provincial town of Cotija, came to Mexico City after almost a decade spent in Culiacán, where he practiced as a contractor. His former partner Santiago Greenham introduced him to the newly developed Jardines del Pedregal that Barragán had created and funded with the Bustamante brothers, but had already abandoned by 1952. Though he had only completed the first year of engineering school, Artigas became a self-taught master builder, a trade he was able to refine through his Pedregal commissions. As he had no formal architectural education, his passion for the machine, especially cars and ships—he initially wanted to become a naval architect—and his travels through California, where he became acquainted with the West Coast landscape, combined with his affinity with the current Brazilian trends led by Oscar Niemeyer and Lucio Costa, comprised his core aesthetic influence. His progressive approach was undoubtedly reinforced by the well-established modern style in Mexico. His private house on Prior Street in San Angel, near Pedregal, exemplifies his desire to bring together natural and man-made elements, and was a prelude to his prolific work in the neighboring development. The lightness achieved by the clean horizontal lines of elongated slabs of exposed concrete and glass walls would become the architect's leitmotif. Artigas's adaptation of the industrialized aesthetic of the California Case Study Houses to this rock-strewn landscape, and his

の時期の3番目のプロジェクトである，コロニア・イポドロモ・デ・ラ・コンデーサのメキシコ公園に面した棟続きになった対のタウンハウスは，セラーノが同じ地域で最初に参加してからほぼ10年後に建てられ，その当時，この辺りは流行エリアで需要の多い地区であったため，密度を最大限にすることが要求された。前述したように，モダン・スタイルは一方では中流と上流階級をターゲットとした製品であり，プロジェクトのコンパクトな性格はおそらく，バラガンがヨーロッパやアメリカへの以前の旅で目にした同時期の作品に触発されたものだろう。当時は既にどの近代都市でも「シンプルな生活」は関心の主流であったのだから。[8] 間口9mの幅の狭い区画に，バラガンは3階建ての住宅2棟を，北側の棟の突き出しを利用して外側に向けて隅窓をつくりだし，公園に向けて最大限の眺めを取り込み，内部空間をより広く見せるために変わった形にして（後に同等にするために変更された），巧みに計画している。ここでもまた，ル・コルビュジエの多面的な影響が，注意深く構成された「自由なファサード」と最上階を屋上庭園として使うというやり方の両方に現れている。バラガンは，ここで早い段階ではあるが，しかし既に洗練された感性を駆使した。つまりそれは，空に開かれた面のダイナミックな相互作用と，1947年，タクバヤの自邸で用いることになる多彩色バージョンのルーフテラスという後年よく使われた手法である。

同じ頃，バラガンは首都の南にある「ペドレガル庭園地区」のためのデザインにあたり，リスクのある大規模開発に既に踏み込み，メキシコのモダニティの前例の無い実験という新しい方向への道を開いていた。コティハの地方都市の出身で，建設業者として経験を積んだクリアカンでほぼ10年を過ごした後，フランシスコ・アルティガス（1916-99年）はメキシコ・シティにやって来た。彼の以前のパートナーであるサンティアゴ・グリーナムが，既に1952年に放棄されていたが，ブスタマンテ兄弟が資金を供給しバラガンが着手して新しく開発されたペドレガル公園をアルティガスに紹介したのである。工科学校の1学年を終了しただけであったが，アルティガスは独学の建築家となった。ペドレガルでの仕事を通して磨くことのできた職業である。彼は正式な建築教育は受けていなかったが，機械，特に車や船に対する情熱——最初は，造船技士になりたいと考えていた——そしてウエスト・コーストの風景に精通することになったカリフォルニアを巡る旅は，オスカー・ニーマイヤーとルシオ・コスタが率いた最新のブラジルの流行に対する親近感と結びついて，彼の受けた美的影響の中心を構成することになった。アルティガスの進歩的な手法は，疑いなく，メキシコに十分に確立された近代様式によって強化された。ペドレガルに近い，サン・アンヘルのプリオール通りに面した自邸は，自然と人工の要素を一つにまとめたいという彼の願いをよく示し，近隣地域の開発での実り豊かな作品群の先駆けとなった。剥き出しのコンクリートの長く延ばされたスラブとガラス壁がつくりだす簡潔な水平線から生まれる軽快さは，この建築家のテーマとなるだろう。カリフォルニアのケース・スタディ・ハウスの工業化された美学の，岩が散乱する風景へのアルティガスの適合の

use of available local craftsmanship, gave rise to the most influential residential trend of the period. Built predominantly for wealthy clients, it came to be known as the Pedregal Style. Members of the next generation such as Antonio Attolini and José María Buendía became prolific followers of his, and adapted their design approach in response to a less affluent yet professional clientele.

By the end of the 1940's the modern trend had become a fashion more than an idealistic movement, and several of its key architectural practitioners were turning to their traditional, even provincial, origins. Barragán's five-year hiatus after his spiritually wearing 'commercial epoch' had triggered a new vision inspired by the traditional buildings of his native Jalisco. His initiative to diverge from mainstream international modernism and retreat into a compositionally massive, rustic and introverted approach, expressed in his private house in Tacubaya and his urban project for El Pedregal, was a historic move that later inspired generations of architects. Almost simultaneously his old-time colleague, the otherwise clean-cut modernist Enrique del Moral (1906-87), built his own house with a similar approach on a nearby lot in Tacubaya (1947). Del Moral, who was also a former pupil and employee of Villagrán's, developed a language based on an early Miesian convergence of horizontal and vertical planes in a rustic local interpretation composed of adobe, brick block, and local volcanic stone, as well as vividly painted rustic stucco walls and exposed concrete slabs.

Eventually, once devoted functionalists such as Yañez, Alberto T. Arai, and O'Gorman himself, turned their backs on pure function and recurred to historical, provincial and traditional sources for inspiration. Yañez's own house, built in El Pedregal (1957-58), is inherently modern in its conception of space but instilled with prehispanic Mixteca-inspired cornices and pattern surfaces. An avowed socialist, his argument for building his own dwelling in luxurious Pedregal was that it offered 'an opportunity to express the nationalistic qualities of architecture in a uniquely enabling place'.

In the mid-1950's, at the peak of Artigas's professional career, his brother criticized his architecture as being 'cold', and as a result he headed toward a stagy provincial rancho style of architecture, and eventually completely abandoned his celebrated modern style. By the end of the sixties, Attolini and Buendía, having developed their own respective progressive reputations in Pedregal, became Barragán's supporters as well, inspired also by the provincial towns of their childhoods. Finally, O'Gorman, as radical when aged as when young, regretted 'not having paid attention to Wright earlier, and instead went for the machinism of Le Corbusier', and built himself another house near Pedregal, in neighboring San Jerónimo between 1947 and 1950, contemporary of Barragán and Del Moral's own houses, this time in a fantastic, grotesque style. He even-

させ方，そして地元で可能な職人技術の使い方はこの時期，最も影響力のある住宅トレンドを生み出した。主に富裕なクライアントのために建てられ，それはペデレガル・スタイルとして知られるようになる。アントニオ・アットリーニやホセ・マリア・ブエンディアのような次世代の所員は，彼の実り多い後継者となり，アルティガスのクライアントほど豊かではないが専門職の顧客に対応して彼らのデザイン手法を適合させた。

1940年代の終わり，モダン・トレンドは，理想主義運動というよりも流行となり，その主要な建築家の幾人かは，伝統的な，地方的でさえある源泉へ向きを変えた。精神的に消耗していた「コマーシャル・エポック」の後，5年間のバラガンの中断は，故郷であるハリスコ州の伝統建築に刺激された新しい構想を誘発することになった。インターナショナル・モダニズムの主流から分かれ，そしてタクバヤの自邸とエル・ペデレガルのための都市計画に表現された，マッシブで，簡潔な，内向する手法による構成への退却という決断は，後に幾世代もの建築家を触発する歴史的動きとなった。ほとんど同時期に，彼の昔の仲間であり，他の点では明白なモダニストであるエンリケ・デル・モラル (1906-87年) は，タクバヤのバラガン自邸近くの土地に同じような手法の自邸を建てた。ビジャグランの以前の生徒でもあり，事務所員であったデル・モラルは，水平な面と垂直な面という初期ミース派の収束点に基づいたランゲージを，日干し煉瓦，煉瓦ブロック，地元の火山岩や鮮やかな色に塗られた荒削りなスタッコ壁や露出されたコンクリート・スラブで構成した，素朴で，地元に根ざした解釈によって展開させた。

結局，ヤニェス，アルベルト・T・アライ，そしてオゴルマン自身といったかつての献身的な機能主義者たちは，純粋な機能主義に背を向けて，インスピレーションを求めて，歴史的，地方的，伝統的源泉に立ち返った。エル・ペデレガルに建てられたヤニェスの自邸 (1957-58年) は空間のコンセプトにおいては本来的にモダンだが，プレ・ヒスパニック時代のミステク族の建物に触発されたコーニスや表面のパターンが吹き込まれている。社会主義者を自認する彼の，贅沢な地区であるペデレガルに自邸を建てる論拠は，「固有の力を持つ場所に，建築の民族主義的特質を表現する機会」を提供するというものだった。

1950年代半ば，アルティガスの専門家としてのキャリアが頂点にあったとき，兄弟からその建築を「冷たい」ものであると批判された結果，彼は芝居がかった地方の小農場スタイル（ランチョ・スタイル）に向かい，結局は賞賛されてきた自身の近代様式を完全に放棄してしまった。同様に，60年代の終わり，ペデレガルで，それぞれに進歩的な建築家としての評判を得ていたアットリーニとブエンディアは，彼らもまた子供時代を過ごした地方の町から刺激を受けて，バラガンの支持者となった。最後に，歳をとっても若い頃と同じように急進的であったオゴルマンは，「もっと以前からフランク・ロイド・ライトに注目していなかったこと。そして，その代わりにル・コルビュジエの機械主義に向かったこと」を後悔し，ペデレガルの近くのサン・ヘロニモ地区に，1947年から1950年にかけて，バ

tually sold the house before he died in 1982.

As is evident from the process by which the house was transformed in Mexico, the urgent necessities that emerged at the end of the Mexican revolution of 1910 catalyzed change in building practices so rapidly that within a few decades the pace of progressive architecture found itself in a sort of reversed course. The modern formula had been so readily self-imposed and so rapidly exhausted that architects once considered radical encountered a different kind of urgency, this time in the impulse to rediscover their origins. In Mexico, what eventually evolved was a reactionary change of approach, a 'mid-life crisis' that proved especially dramatic because of its appearance soon after a modernity that seemed the only true and honest way for an entire generation. By the middle of the century the term 'revolution', as it had been understood two decades before, was to be revised.

(1) Antonin Artaud, various conferences during his visit to Mexico, 1936. Antonin Artaud, Mensajes Revolucionarios, Textos Sobre México. Editorial Letras Vivas. México, 2000, p. 94
(2) Acevedo was a well-traveled and cultured young architect who was influenced by the writings of nineteenth-century French theorists, and had introduced to the Mexican academy, and the architectural community in general, the works by Cloquet. He joined the branch offices in Mexico of Emile Benard, and independently entered several competitions, for all of which he won the first prize, though none were ever built. Published in 1920, two years after his early death at 36, was Disertaciones de un Arquitecto, a compilation of his influential lectures from as early as 1908 that accounted for his progressive thoughts, in which he already insinuated the idea of 'necessity' as the basis for form, and yearned for a new architecture based on the use of new materials such as steel and reinforced concrete
(3) President Carranza's government (1915-20) contributed to the tendency toward proliferation by decreeing a tax exemption for all houses built in the Colonial style. The derivative mannerisms of this aesthetic, called California Colonial, were to develop in parallel and play the role of rival to modern architecture for the next three decades
(4) José Antonio Cuevas, a prominent engineer who taught structural stability at the School of Architecture, and who was later to become one of Juan O'Gorman's influential teachers, had built between 1921 and 1929 more than sixty buildings using reinforced concrete
(5) 'Approximately 15% of construction is in the hands of architects'. I. E. Myers, Mexico's Modern Architecture. Architectural Book Publishing Co., Inc. New York. 1952, p. 49
(6) Israel Katzaman, Arquitectura Contemporánea Mexicana, INAH/ SEP, 1964, p. 102
(7) Esther Born. The New Architecture in Mexico. The Architectural Record/ William Morrow and Company. New York, 1937, p. 3
(8) Esther Born. The New Architecture in Mexico. The Architectural Record/ William Morrow and Company. New York, 1937, p. 78

ラガンとデル・モラル，それぞれの自邸と同時代に，もう一つの家を，今度は空想的なグロテスク様式で自ら建設したが，結局，彼は，1982年に亡くなる前に売却した。

メキシコにおける住宅の変遷のプロセスから明らかなように，1910年のメキシコ革命の終わりに出現した急を要する状況は，建設の仕事における変化をあまりに急速に押し進めたため，数十年の間に，進歩的な建築の歩調は一種の逆行コースに入ってしまった。近代的な公式を，あまりに容易に自らに課し，あまりに急速に消耗しつくし，かつて急進的と見なされた建築家は，革命時とは異なる種類の緊急性，今度は彼らのルーツを再発見する衝動に直面した。とどのつまりメキシコにおいて生まれたものは，方法の反動的変化であり，すべての世代にとって唯一の真実で正しい方法であると見えたモダニティのすぐあとに続いて現れたために，ひとしお劇的なものとなった「中年の危機」であった。20世紀の半ばには，20年前に理解されていたものとしての「革命」という言葉は，修正を余儀なくされた。

（1）アントナン・アルトー，1936年の彼のメキシコ訪問中には様々な会議が開かれた。Antonin Artaud, "Mensajes Revolucionarios（革命のメッセージ）"よりメキシコについての抜粋。Editorial Letras Vivas刊, México, 2000, p.94
（2）アセベドは19世紀フランスの理論家の著作に影響を受けた，よく旅をし，洗練された教養のある若い建築家で，メキシコの学界や建築界全般にクロケの作品を紹介した。エミール・ベナールのメキシコ支部に加わり，個人的にいくつかの設計競技に応募，そのすべてで1等賞を得たが，そのどれもが実際に建てられることはなかった。36歳という若さでの死の2年後，1920年に出版された『ある建築家の論述』は，彼の進歩的な考え方を明らかにする，早くも1908年から強い影響力を及ぼした講義を編集したもので，その中で彼は既に，形態の基礎として「必要性」という考えをそれとなく浸透させ，スティールや鉄筋コンクリートなどの新しい材料の使用に基づいた新しい建築を切望している
（3）カランサス大統領の政権（1915-20年）は，コロニアル・スタイルで建てられたすべての住宅に対する税控除の法令を定めることによって，それを急増させる方向へ向かわせた。カリフォルニア・コロニアルと呼ばれるこの美学の誘導されたマンネリズムは，次の30年間，近代建築に並行して発展し，そのライバルとしての役割を演じた
（4）建築大学で構造の安定性を教えた卓越したエンジニアであり，後にオゴルマンに深い影響を与えた教師となったホセ・アントニオ・クエバスは，1921年から1929年にかけて，鉄筋コンクリートを使用した建物を60以上建てている
（5）「建物の約15%が建築家の手になるものである」。I. E. Myers, "Mexico's Modern Architecture", Architectural Book Publishing Co., Inc. New York, 1952, p.49
（6）Israel Katzaman, "Architectura Contemporanea Mexicana", INAH/SEP, 1964, p.102
（7）Esther Born,"The New Architecture in Mexico", Architectural Record/William Morrow and Company, New York, 1937, p. 3
（8）前掲書, p. 78

Juan O'Gorman Diego Rivera and Frida Kahlo House-Studio

Mexico City, Mexico, 1932

Overall view from south: Rivera's house on left, Kahlo's house on right　南側全景：左はリベラの家，右はカーロの家

Rivera's house　リベラの家

Cantilevered staircase of Kahlo's house　カーロの家，片持ちの外階段

Spiral staircase of Rivera's house　リベラの家の螺旋階段

This is a house with an atelier for Diego Rivera and Frida Kahlo, standing in San Angel district where used to be the outskirts of Mexico City at the time when the building was constructed. Each space for Rivera and Kahlo was independently placed, while Rivera's house painted in white and reddish-brown and Kahlo's house painted in vivid blue were connected by the bridge across the roofs to clearly represent the relationship of the two. As if the spaces reflect the activity levels of Rivera and Kahlo, the house of Rivera is slightly larger than Kahlo's (In plan, the house of Rivera is in 8 x 12 m, and the house of Kahlo is in 6 x 6 m). The thin concrete columns standing in grid manner are holding up the entire buildings, while the ceilings are waffled slabs with concrete frames to fix bricks in checked pattern. This system is commonly utilized for both houses.

Juan O'Gorman completed this house in 1932, and the European modernism had been already brought to Mexico at that time. Although this piece of work appears to have received strong influence from Le Corbusier, it has a uniqueness to its usage of a compact unit as a module, which is different from the one often applied in Europe. Furthermore, this house has an important aspect as it reflects the facts—that the concept of polychromy was linked together with the colorful Mexican culture to bring in the vivid usage of colors into modernism; the time period was not too different from the construction of Villa Savoye in 1931 by Corbusier—the modernism in Mexico had already achieved a unique localization in 1930's based on the Mexican culture as a background, and started to show different kind of development.

Later on in 1956, O'Gorman completed his private house in completely opposite concept, covered up with the mosaic of raw stones of Mexico—the return of this architect to the house that makes us strongly feel the influence of the native Mexican's culture. It tells a story of how the background of this country is bold as a culture. In that sense, the house of Rivera and Kahlo can be said as an epoch-making product revealing the frontier of pure modernism, tried to establish itself in the land of Mexico.

竣工当時はメキシコ・シティの郊外であった，サン・アンヘル地区に建つ，ディエゴ・リベラとフリーダ・カーロの住宅兼アトリエ。二人の空間は独立して置かれ，白と赤褐色で塗られたリベラの家と鮮やかな青色のカーロの家は，屋上に架けられたブリッジでつながれ，二人の関係性が明快に表現されている。それぞれの活動を反映するかのように，リベラの家はカーロのそれより少し大きい（平面形では，リベラの家は8×12メートル，カーロの家は6×6メートル）。グリッド状に立つ細いコンクリート柱が全体を支え，天井は，格子状に並べたレンガの周囲をコンクリートで固めたワッフルスラブ。そのシステムは二つの家に共通している。

ホアン・オゴルマンがこの家を完成させたのは1932年。この時代，すでにヨーロッパのモダニズムがメキシコには持ち込まれていた。特にコルビュジエの影響を強く感じさせるこの作品は，しかしながらモデュールがヨーロッパのそれとは異なり，かなりコンパクトなユニットが用いられている点は特徴である。さらに，ポリクロミーのコンセプトがメキシコの色彩文化と結びつくことで，鮮やかな色使いをモダニズムに持ち込んだこと，これが出来たのが，コルビュジエがサヴォア邸を建てた1931年とさほど変わらない時期であることを考えると，すでに1930年代に，モダニズムがメキシコの文化を背景を元に独自なローカリゼーションを成し，別の展開を見せていたのであり，そこにこの住宅の重要な意味がある。

その後，オゴルマンは，1956年，この住宅とは対極的に異なる，メキシコの原石のモザイクで埋め尽くされた自邸をつくることとなる。建築家の，メキシコ先住民族の文化の影響を強く感じさせるこの家への回帰。この国のバックグラウンドがいかに強大な文化であったかを物語る。その意味で，リベラとカーロの家は，メキシコに根付こうとしたピュア・モダニズムの先陣が垣間見えるエポック・メイキングな存在と言えるだろう。

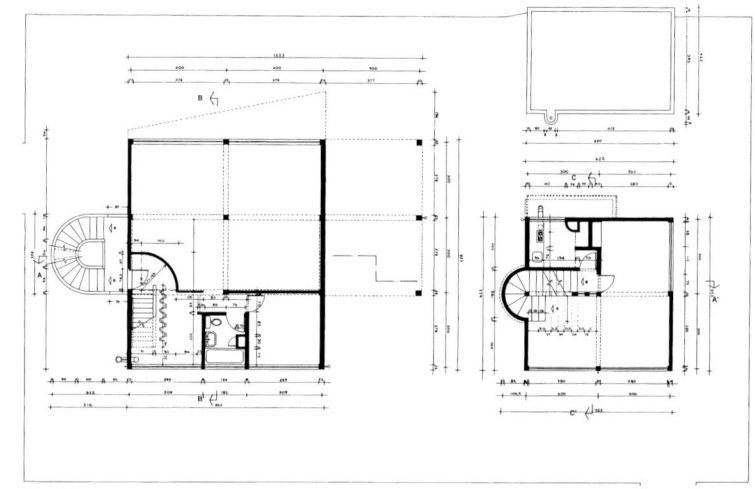

First floor

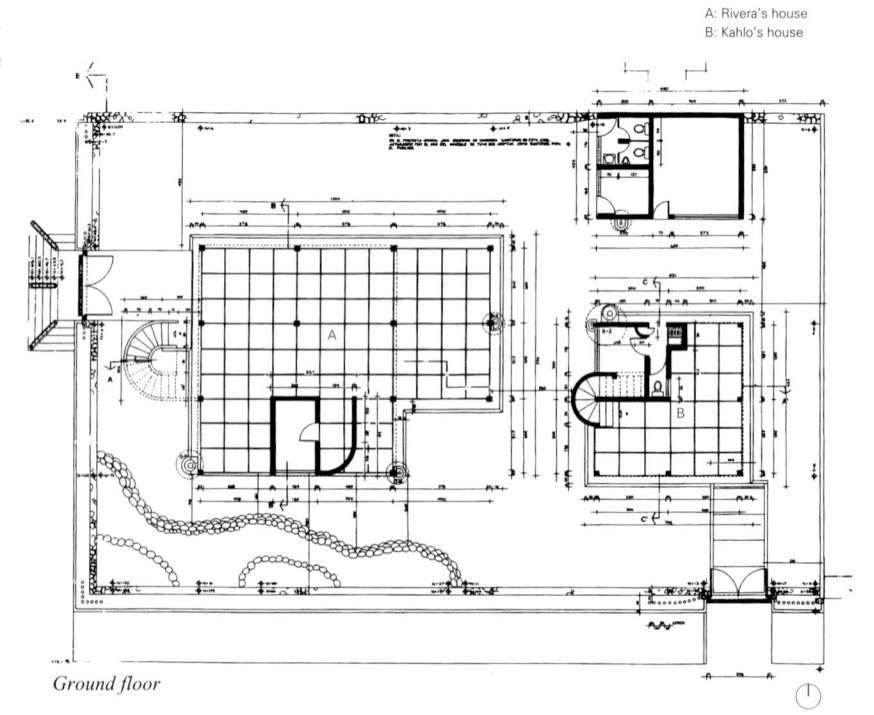

A: Rivera's house
B: Kahlo's house

Ground floor

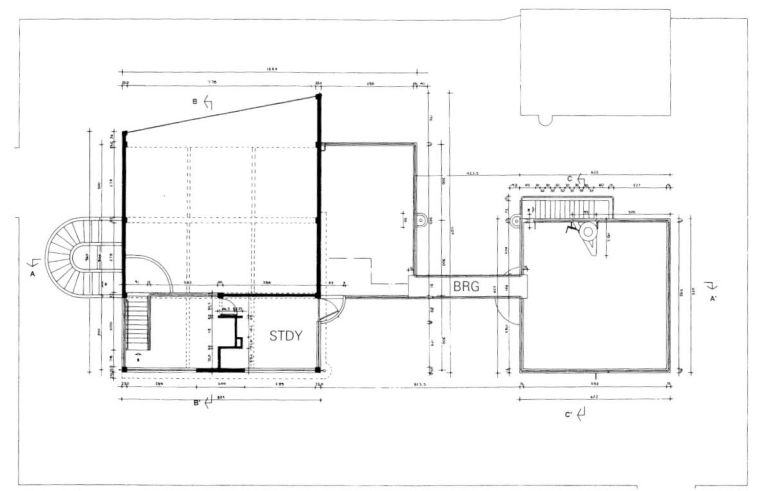

Third floor

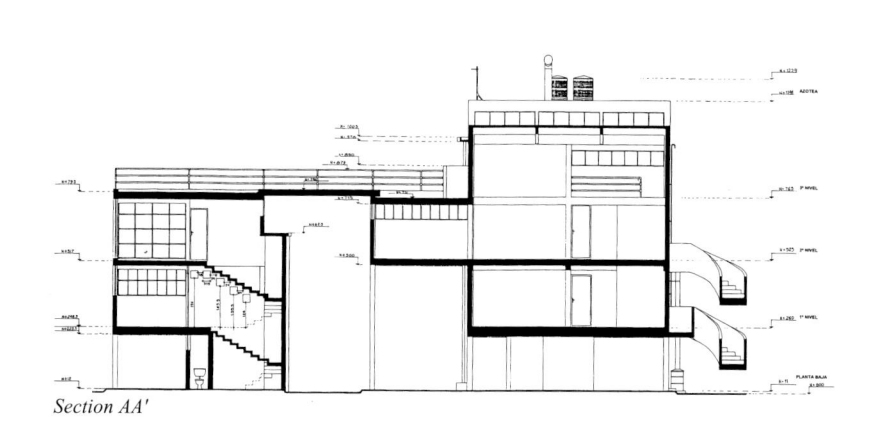

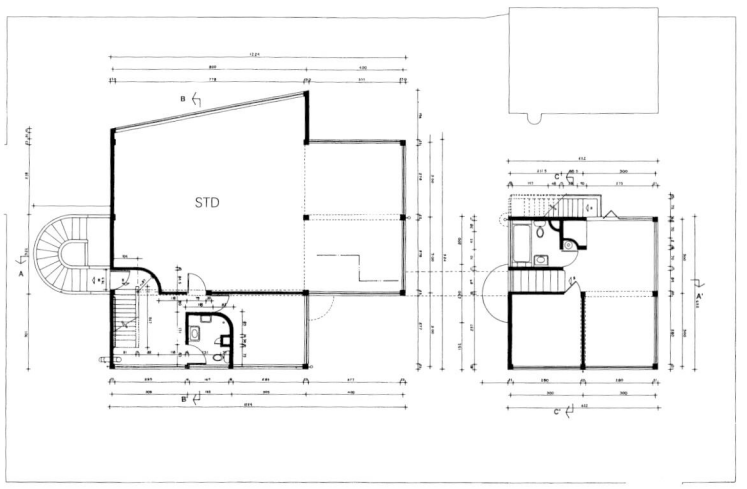

Section AA'

Second floor

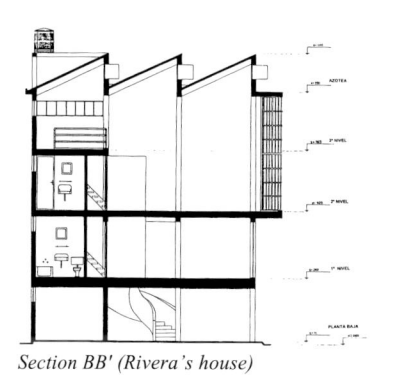

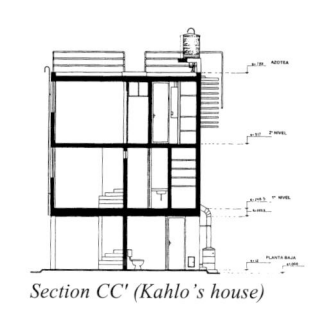

Section BB' (Rivera's house)

Section CC' (Kahlo's house)

Pilotis of Rivera's house: view toward entrance gate on west リベラの家，ピロティ：西側のエントランス・ゲートを見る

Annex of Kahlo's house: originally used as studio of Guillermo Kahlo (Frida's father)
カーロの家，離れ：ギジェルモ・カーロ（フリーダの父）のスタジオとして使われていた

View from pilotis of Rivera's house toward Kahlo's house　リベラの家のピロティよりカーロの家を見る

Pilotis of Rivera's house: protruded white cube as studio from Rivera's house toward Kahlo's house
リベラの家，ピロティ：上の白いヴォリュームは，リベラの家からカーロの家に向かって突き出たスタジオ部分

Roof terrace with bridge between two houses: view from Kahlo's toward Rivera's house　２つの家を結ぶブリッジのあるルーフ・テラス：カーロの家からリベラの家を見る

Spiral staircase of Rivera's house leading to studio on second floor　３階のスタジオへ続くリベラの家の螺旋階段

Rivera's house: studio on second floor リベラの家，3階のスタジオ

Kahlo's house, second floor カーロの家，3階

Rivera's house: staircase on second floor　リベラの家，3階の階段

Rivera's house: entrance on second floor　リベラの家：3階，外の螺旋階段からの入口

Rivera's house, first floor　リベラの家，2階

Kahlo's house, first floor　カーロの家，2階

◁△*Staircase of Kahlo's house*　カーロの家：階段室

Juan O'Gorman Architect's House

Mexico City, Mexico, 1956

Bedroom: view from east 寝室のヴォリューム：東より見る

Roof garden: skylight of living room on right 屋上庭園：右は居間のトップライト

Entrance 玄関

O'Gorman has been following two paths at the same time in his life, one of a painter and the other of an architect who designed such as the Mexico University Library and the painter Frida Kahlo and Diego Rivera's house, but has spent his last years working mainly as painter.

His own house stands on the lava ground of Pedregal, in the vicinity of the university campus. It is covered with stone mosaic of Mexican origin. Mythological shapes and figures out of Mayan and Aztec civilizations fill the entirety of the house.

In fact, O'Gorman admits himself that this idea of stone mosaic had to do with his father being a mining engineer. Back in his childhood, he had been familiar with the rare samples of mineral rocks that his father would bring home. The interior is finished with the same lava and mosaic as the exterior. A streak of light from the ceiling creates a mystical mood inside the semi-darkness of the room, inducing a false illusion of being inside a lava cave. There are no walls to partition the room which integrates the bedroom connected to the living room one flight down through a set of stairs. Together with the dry atmosphere and the vegetation who has found its way into the room, the space provides a unique, primitive and yet soothing experience.
Makoto Suzuki

オゴルマンは画家と建築家の二つの道を生涯歩み、晩年はほとんど画家として活動していた。建築作品としては、「メキシコ大学図書館」と「フリーダ・カーロとディエゴ リベラの家」などを残している。

大学都市の近く、ペドレガルの溶岩地帯に建つこの自邸は、メキシコで産する原石のモザイクで埋められており、マヤ文明やアステカ文明から生まれた神話の形象が家全体を覆っている。

実はこの石のモザイクのアイディアは、彼の父が鉱山技師であったことから生まれたと本人が語っている。子供の頃から家には父親が持ち帰る珍しい鉱石のサンプルがあったらしい。室内は外観と同じ仕上げの溶岩とモザイクで、天井から指す一条の光が、薄暗い室内に神秘的な雰囲気を醸しだし、溶岩の穴のなかにいるような錯覚を起こす。室内の区切りはなく、階下の居間と階段でつながっている寝室とは一体になっており、部屋のなかまで進出している植物、乾燥した空気と共に、原始的な落ち着いた他では経験することのできない空間である。
（鈴木恂）

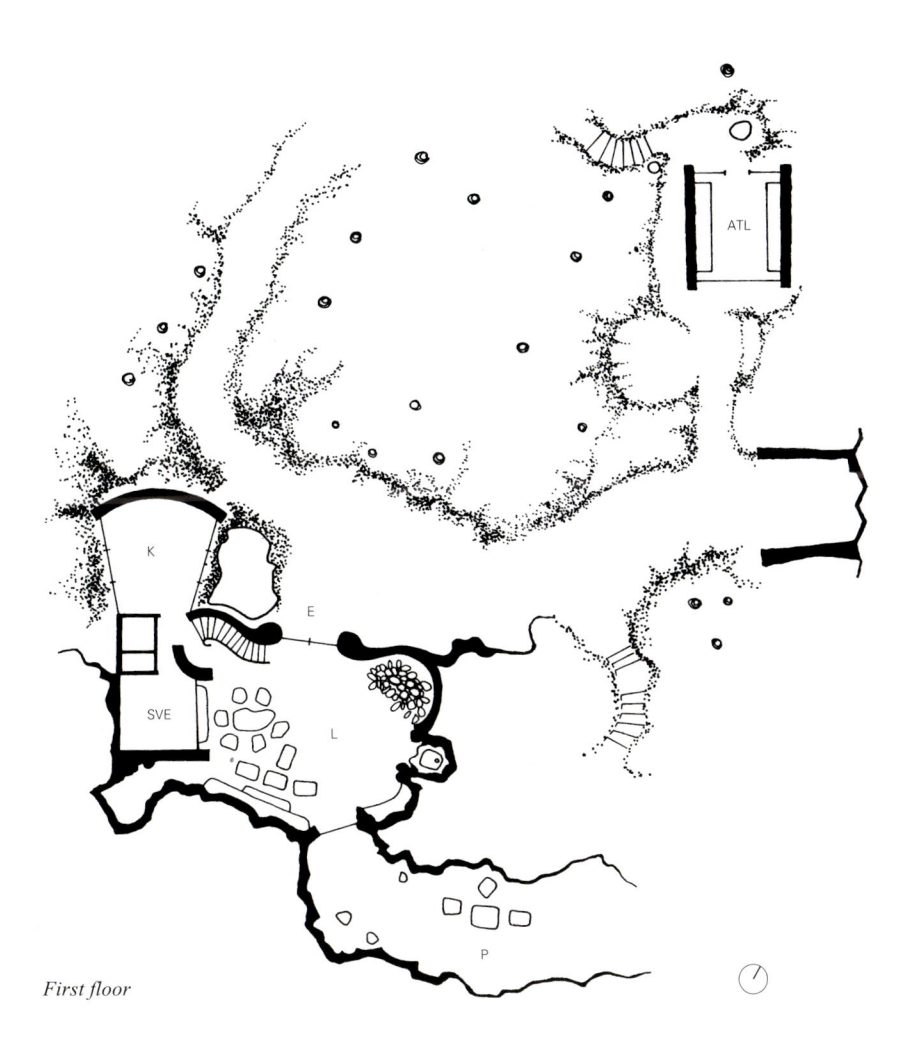

Trrace on second floor 2階のテラス

Atelier アトリエ△▽

First floor

△▽*Living room*　居間

Ceiling of staircase　階段室の天井

Living room 居間

Luis Barragán   Barragán House
Mexico City, Mexico, 1947

Street view 通りより見る

Hall ホール

Living room: looking garden 居間：庭を見る

Living room 居間

The site is situated in the southwestern part of downtown Mexico City, in the same neighborhood that Barragán had sold in lots in 1940s. He has designed several buildings, one of which is this private house of his own. The house faces a quiet narrow street, some steps away from the boulevard. Its exterior is characterized by a facade with few openings but a huge square window. The only landmark is the white tower that rises on rooftop.

Barragán has worked on the house's reform and maintenance a number of times, as it is often the case with most other architects with their own residences, and has tailored it to satisfy his constant search for a comfortable space of perfect beauty. The rooftop garden consisting solely of colored walls and tower captures the blue sky of Mexico. It is a silent space, secluded from the outside world.

One enters the modest, dimly-lit entrance from a calm street and opens the door that gives to a hall. Stairs paved with volcanic rocks; sunlight finding its way from the window above; walls painted separately in white and pink; built-in telephone table; black persimmon chair as a refined piece of Mexican traditional folk craft; a painting of shimmering gold. Every single element that composes this space has kept an impeccable harmony since the master had left this house, and the space's perfect proportion continues to impress the visitors, purifying their senses. Further into the house await spaces for meditation and escape from everyday life—the living room and the study that were created to serve the architect himself.

敷地はメキシコ・シティの南西部の下町に位置する。バラガンは1940年代，この一帯を分譲し，幾つかの建物を設計したが，その一つがこの自邸である。大通りより一歩入った静かな細い通りに面した外観は正方形の大窓があるだけの開口部の少ないファサードで，屋上にそびえる白い塔が唯一の目印となる。

他の建築家の自邸同様，バラガンはこの家を幾度となく改築，手を入れ，彼の求め続けた居心地の良い，完璧な美の空間に仕立て上げた。彩色された壁と塔だけで構成される屋上庭園はメキシコの青空を切り取り，外界と遮断された静寂の空間である。

人通りの少ない通りから質素で薄暗い玄関を入り，次のドアを開けるとホールに出る。火山岩の敷かれた階段，その上の窓から射し込む陽光，白とピンク色に塗り分けられた壁，造り付けの電話のテーブルと，メキシコの伝統民芸をリファインした黒柿の椅子，金色に輝く一枚の絵。この空間を構成するすべてのエレメントは主無き今日でも完璧な調和を保ち，その空間の完璧なプロポーションはいつでも感動を与えてくれる。この空間で感覚を浄化された後，さらに建築家自身のための，日常からの逃避と沈思の場，リビング・ルームと書斎が控えている。

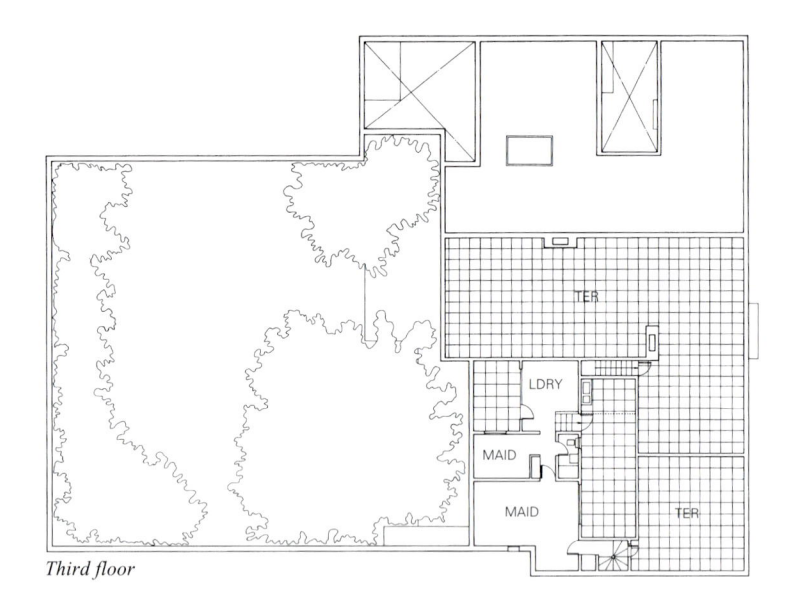

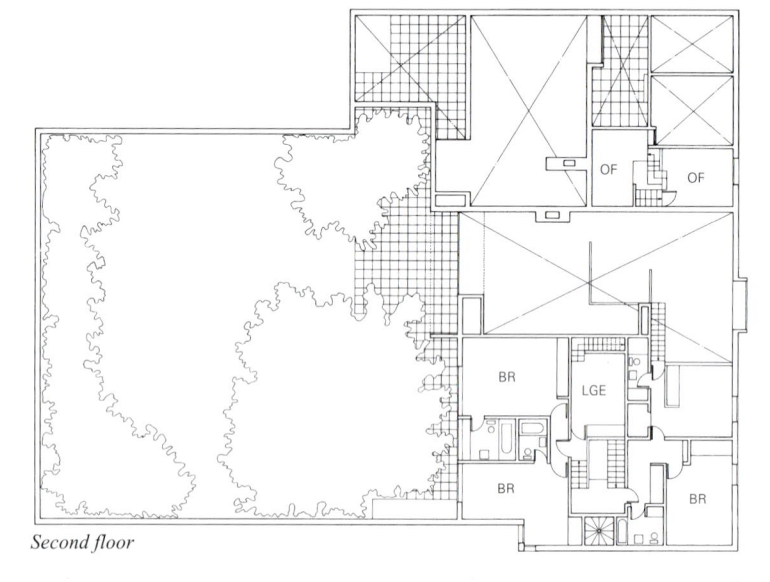

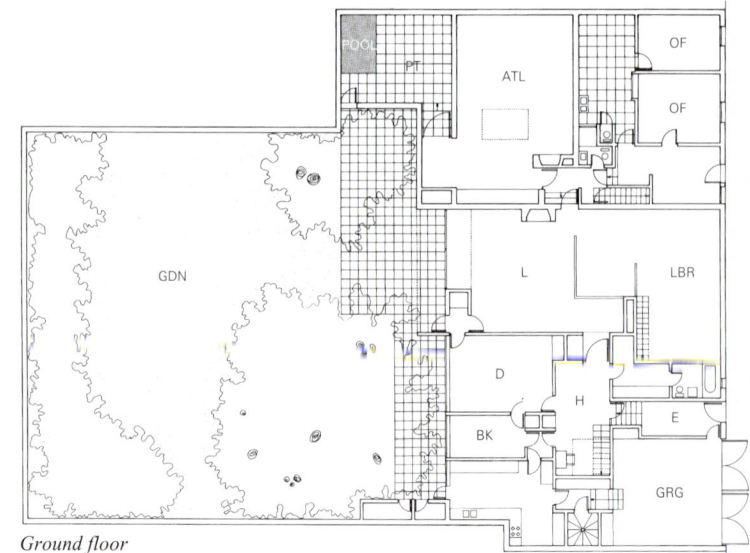

Third floor

Second floor

Ground floor

View toward living room from garden　庭より居間を見る

Living room 居間

Staircase in library 書庫の階段

Study in bedroom 寝室脇の書斎机

Bedroom 寝室

Roof terrace 屋上テラス

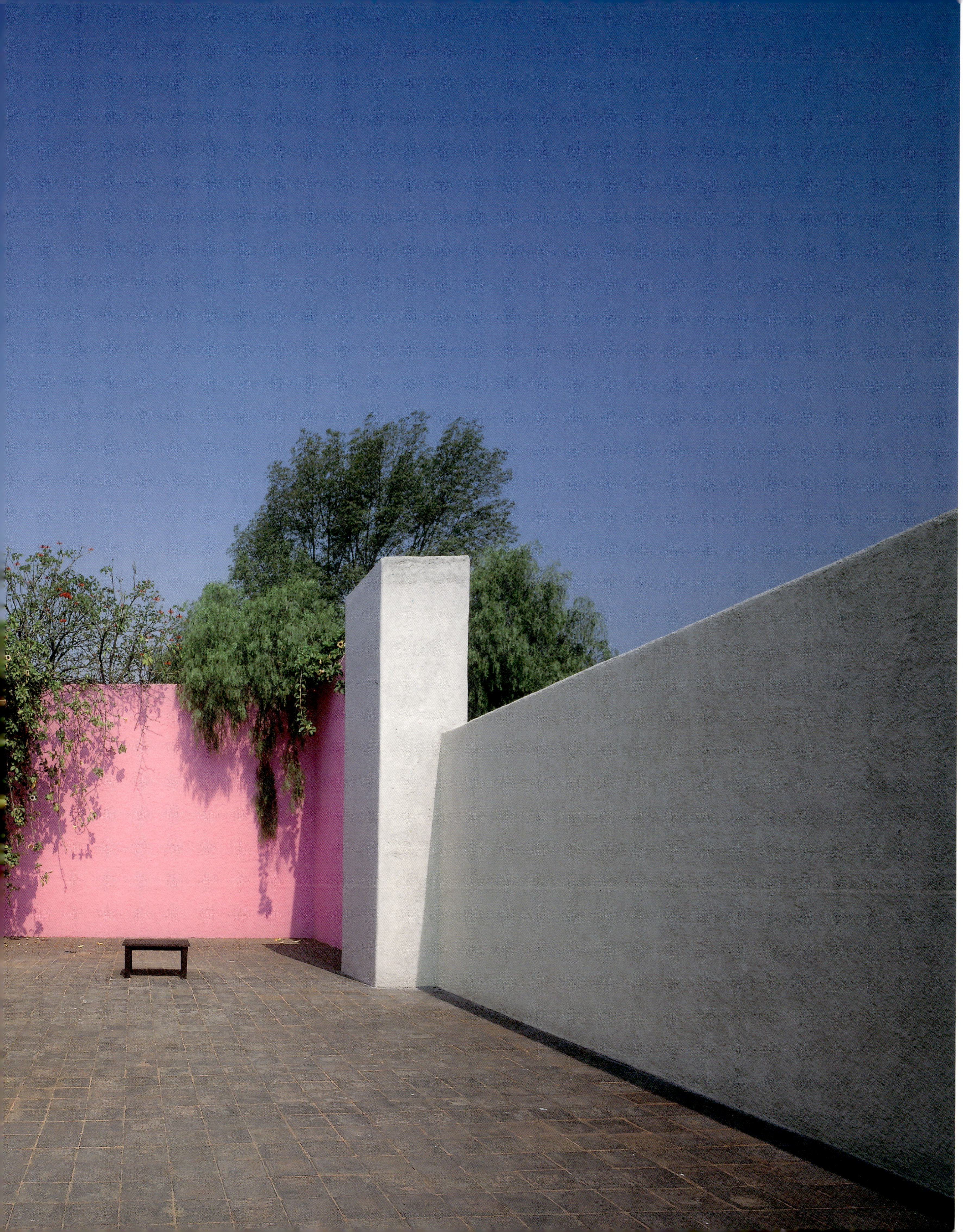

Patio 中庭

View toward patio from atelier アトリエより中庭を見る

Max Ludwig Cetto   Cetto House

Mexico City, Mexico, 1948–51

Overall view from west garden　西側の庭より見る

View from east garden　東側の庭より見る

Max Ludwig Cetto was born on February 20, 1903 in Köblenz, Germany. He was formed as an architect in Berlin since 1923, under the tutelage of the expressionist Hans Poelzig. From Berlin he moved to Frankfurt am Main, immediately after finishing his studies with Poelzig, where he collaborated in the great urban-architectonic enterprise of the Frankfurt Works Department, under the helm of Ernst May, in that consummated utopia according Manfredo Tafuri. Cetto was a key piece within the office's architectural design department since 1926 and until its dissolution in 1930 making small buildings for the city's electric company. Even today you can find these interventions by Cetto throughout all the city of Frankfurt.

Cetto's experience in the German architectonic environment of the time would be a fundamental key for his later reflections upon his arrival to Mexico; during this time in Germany he met Walter Gropius, Le Corbusier, Ludwig Hilberseimer, and Sigfried Giedion, among others, the latter will invite him to participate in the CIAM (International Congress of Modern Architecture) after knowing and praising his project in the 1927 competition for the Palace of the League of Nations, in Geneva, the same competition with that rare judgment given by the jury against Le Corbusier that detonated that unprecedented union among modern architects into the CIAM. Thus, within this crucible of modernity, Max Cetto was nurtured by the new architecture and the new objectivity.

Max Cetto migrated to Mexico in 1939 after a brief stay in the United States where he visited Walter Gropius. Later, still in the United States, he met Frank Lloyd Wright at his office in Taliesin where he remained for several weeks; Wright's architecture always had affected Max Cetto profoundly. Few weeks after Wright would recommend Cetto to work for Richard Neutra in California, where he worked directly in the supervision of the Sydney Kahn House.

Max Cetto and the First Architecture for El Pedregal; Tradition and Modernity

The influence of Wright's architecture in the work of Cetto is undeniable; Cetto himself would speak of his experience in

Taliesin as fundamental; the organicism in the 'Kaufmann House' (Pennsylvania 1936) and its material relation with the landscape, and the confrontation with the desert environment proposed in the 'Pauson House' (Phoenix 1940), are the subjects of the wrightian project where Max Cetto would put more attention.

In Mexico, Cetto collaborated since 1939 and for nearly 10 years with Luis Barragán. It is possible to highlight from this period the work of Cetto related to the outlining of a feasible architecture in the urban development known as El Pedregal, both, ideologically and constructively. In the two "display houses" on the Avenue Las Fuentes, No. 130 and 140 respectively, is possible to observe the elements that will detonate a unique architecture, native from the site but modern at the same time, the long flattened walls, the free and abstract stairways, the squared proportion windows overlooking the garden and points of interest.

Early at the beginning when Max Cetto works with Barragán in El Pedregal, he accomplishes to buy a terrain inside the housing complex, on Agua Street, the number 130, a lot of 1,800 m² approximately. In this place, Cetto builds his own house, the first one to be finished in El Pedregal de San Ángel (1949).

The house is built with materials from the place, traditional, but used in a modern way, the wood, the stone, and the steel. The used of stone as an element that embeds the building to the ground is an architectonic condition very used by Germans, who understand the tectonic as belonging to the site, as well as the use of big windows (also used in the Avenue Las Fuentes display houses). The wood as closing element constitutes one of the most traditional construction elements of North America, and the steel and concrete as super-structure would became the material that lead to the reference of progress and modernity, used in window frames and pergolas.

In this house two stages are distinguished, the first one corresponds to 1949 when Cetto builds the first level, a body at the middle of the plot, remaining surrounded by gardens of exotic flowers and standing above volcanic rock. The second one corresponds to the expansion

Terrace テラス

Entrance from terrace テラスからの入口

as the second level, placing one more room, a bathroom, and the architect's atelier; a glass "box" facing west achieving an extraordinary view of El Pedregal's exuberant landscape. In this work-place is possible to appreciate a mural over the ceiling under the sky deck, built with a great influence of his friend Juan O'Gorman, using colored stones (as in the murals of the University City Central Library) for representing astrologic images and the ideology of the Cetto family.

The Cetto House in El Pedregal constitutes a paradigm of Modern Mexican Architecture from the mid-twentieth century, by its reflection before the landscape and its proposal for mixing tradition and modernity; it is regionalist architecture but with international accents at the same time.

マックス・ルートヴィヒ・チェットは1903年2月20日にドイツのコブレンツに生まれた。彼は，1923年からベルリンで表現主義の建築家ハンス・ペルツィヒの指導により建築家としての修養を積んだ。ペルツィヒのもとでの勉学を終えるとすぐにフランクフルト・アム・マインに移り，エルンスト・マイの指揮下で行われたフランクフルト建設局の，マンフレッド・タフーリによれば完璧なユートピアという非常に優れた都市建築の大事業に加わった。チェットは1926年から組織が解散した1930年まで建築設計部門のなかでの要職にあり，市の電力会社の小規模な建物もいくつかつくっている。今日でも，チェットによるこれらの仕事のあとをフランクフルト市の至る所に見つけることができる。

当時のドイツにおける建築環境の中でのチェットの経験は，後年，メキシコ到着時の考え方の基調を形成したことだろう。ドイツでのこの時期に，彼はウォルター・グロピウス，ル・コルビュジエ，ルートヴィヒ・ヒルベルザイマー，ジークフリート・ギーディオンに出会っている。なかでもギーディオンは，1927年の，ジュネーヴの国際連盟本部設計競技のチェットの案を知り，賞賛した後，彼をCIAM（近代建築国際会議）に参加するように招いた。ル・コルビュジエに反対する審査員によるひどい判定が行われたこの設計競技が，近代建築家たちによる前例のない連合であるCIAMの結

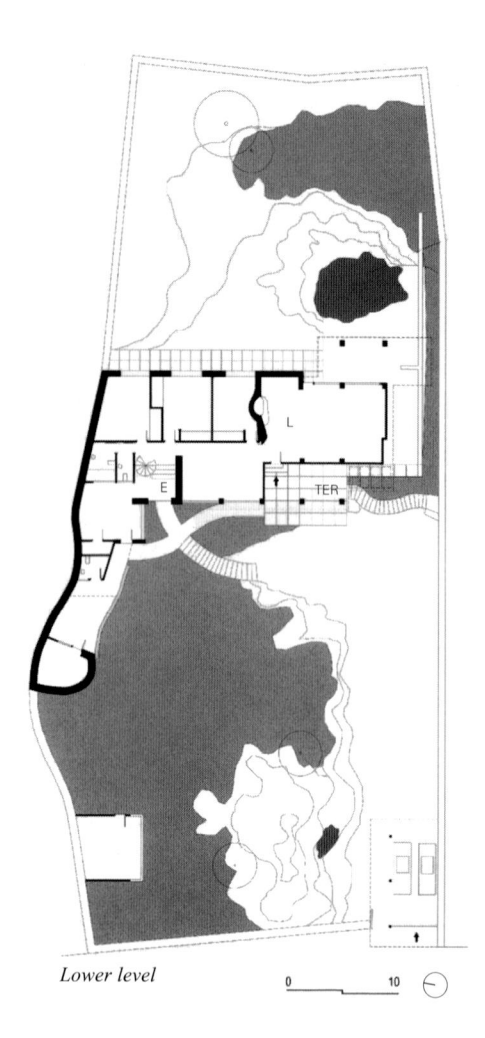

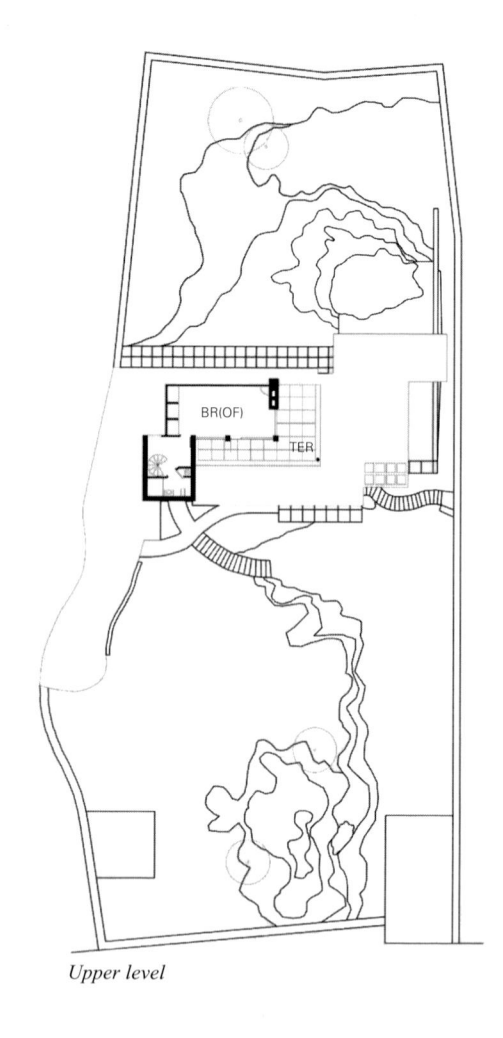

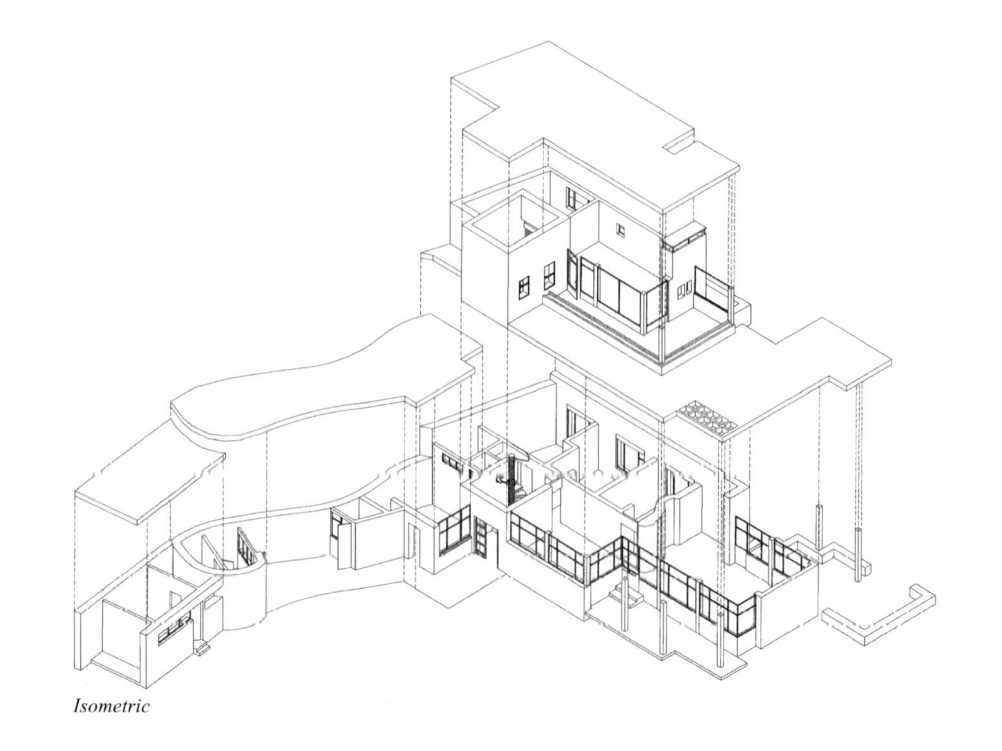

Lower level

Upper level

Isometric

Approach アプローチ

Terrace テラス

Entrance 入口

Spiral staircase made of concrete コンクリート製の螺旋階段

成を触発する契機となった。こうして，この近代性のるつぼの中で，マックス・チェットは新しい建築と新しい客観的精神によって育てられた。

チェットはアメリカ合衆国への短い滞在の後，1939年にメキシコに移住した。合衆国ではウォルター・グロピウスを訪ねた後，タリアセンの事務所でフランク・ロイド・ライトに会い，そこに数週間滞在した。ライトの建築は常にチェットを深く惹き付けた。数週間後，ライトは彼にカリフォルニアのリチャード・ノイトラのもとで働くことを勧め，彼はシドニー・カーン邸を直接，担当することになる。

〈マックス・チェットとエル・ペドレガルの最初の建築：伝統と近代的なもの〉
チェットの作品には，ライトの建築の影響があることは否定できない。チェット自身，タリアセンでの自分の体験を本質的なものであったと述べている。「カフマン邸」（ペンシルベニア，1936年）の有機性や材料の風景とのつながり，そして「ポーソン邸」（フェニックス，1940年）に提案された砂漠の環境との対峙などは，ライトの作品で，チェットがより多くの注意を払った主題である。

メキシコで，チェットは，1939年から10年近くをルイス・バラガンと協働した。この時期以降のチェットの仕事が，エル・ペドレガルとして知られる都市開発に相応しい建築像を構想することに，観念的にも構成的にも関係づけられるということは注目に値する。ラス・フェンテス通りに面した2つの"展示住宅"，No.130とそれに続く140では，独特な建築を触発することになる，この土地のものであり，しかし同時に近代的である諸要素が認められる。たとえば，長く平坦に延びる壁，独立した抽象的な形を持つ階段，庭園や趣のある場所を見晴らせる正方形の比例を持つ窓。

バラガンと共にエル・ペドレガルで仕事を始めたごく初期に，チェットは集合住宅の内側に，約1,800平米のNo.130の区画を購入した。彼はこの場所にエル・ペドレガル・デ・サン・アンヘルで最初に完成した家となる自邸を建てることになる。

この家は，地元の伝統的な材料，木，石，それにスティールを使って，しかし近代的な方法で建てられている。大きな窓の使用（ラス・フェンテス通りの展示住宅でも使われた）や，敷地の地質構造を理解し，建物

Northwest end 北西端部

Terrace on upper level 上階テラス

を地面に嵌め込む要素である石の使い方は，ドイツ人がよく用いる建築術である．建物を包む要素としての木材は北アメリカの最も伝統的な建築要素を構成し，上部構造としてのスティールとコンクリートは，窓枠やパーゴラに使われ，進歩と近代性のレファレンスへと導く材料となるだろう．

この住宅では２つの時期が識別される．最初は1949年，チェットが，魅惑的な花の庭で囲まれ，火山岩の上に立ち上がる１階部分を敷地の中央に建てたときに相当する．第２期に相当するのは２階の増築で，部屋をもう一つと浴室，そして建築家のアトリエが加えられた．西に面したガラス"ボックス"からはエル・ペドレガルの溢れんばかりに豊かな風景の素晴らしい眺めが望める．この仕事場からはスカイデッキの下の天井を覆う壁画も鑑賞できる．これは彼の友人ホアン・オゴルマンの大きな影響下でつくられ，チェット一家の占星術的イメージと空想的な思考を表現するために，着色した石が使われている（「大学都市，中央図書館」の壁画のように）．

エル・ペドレガルのこの住宅は，その風景を重んじる考え，伝統と近代性を混合する提案によって，20世紀半ば以来，近代メキシコ建築の規範を構成するものとなってきた．それはリージョナリストの建築であるが，同時にインターナショナルな特色を備えている．

Office: originally used as bedroom オフィス：元は主寝室として使われていた
Photo by Daniel Escotto▽

Living room 居間

Francisco Artigas & Fernando Luna Rojas House

Mexico City, Mexico, 1962

This is an early work of Francisco Artigas called 'Gomez House' (1951-52). This house is known as his masterpiece and it balances on the existing lava rock cone which is used as a structural element. At the same time this house is significant in terms of becoming the standard typology for housing in Pedregal. This was the first house in the region which made use of seasonal flowers to grow on the coarse lava fields which was believed impossible. Expressing how nature is beautiful—just as it is—has become a guiding principal for the housing that followed, and people in Pedregal have begun to compete to see how well they can bring together the natural beauty of lava and human architectural efforts.

This house expresses these ideas frankly. The main part of this house is laid between a natural cleft in the lava and it consists of two simple and clear horizontal slabs, one floor and one ceiling. This is strongly contrasting to the soft subtle ambiguities of the undulating lava. This simplicity is characteristic of his architecture and most noticeable when seen in section. There are various kinds of spaces on the plan which is achieved by indentations or the curvature of the corridor. However in section the height of the ceiling gives the space an expansive feel and seems to go on forever.

We can experience the lively spaces of the children's rooms designed by Artigas. At his own house (1960) he separated the children's territory completely as they grew up and he built it behind a clump of trees. He gave them an independent patio to mark their territory clearly. We can find a delicate thoughtfulness in these humble gestures which we could never imagine from just viewing his simple structure.

The enjoyment of the approach to this house is one of its most unforgettable characteristics. As I walked up the gentle stairs, I could view the whole family swimming in the generous pool, and this left a lasting impression.
Makoto Suzuki

アルティガスの初期の作品に「ゴメス邸」(1951-52年) という住宅がある。この住宅は溶岩の盛りあがった頂にバランスをとって置かれたような，溶岩を意識的に構造として利用した傑作として知られる。同時に，ペドレガル住宅区の典型をつくり出したという点でも意義深い。草木が生えないとされてきたペドレガルの粗い岩原に，季節の草花をワッと咲かせたのも，この住宅においてであった。自然が，そのままでもいかに美しいものかを表した事は，この後につくられた住宅の信条となったし，ペドレガルの家々は競って溶岩の美しさを建築と結びつける工夫を凝らしたのだ。

この住宅は，そのような意図を実に率直に表現していると思われる。溶岩の裂け目に渡された住居の主な部分は，溶岩の起伏や柔らかな陰影とは対照的に，単純で明快な床と天井の2枚の水平スラブの間に表現されている。こうした単純化は，アルティガスの断面がもつ一つの特徴といえる。平面的にはやや入り組んだ部分や廊下の曲がりによって多様な空間を与えながら，断面では基準となる床と天井の高さがどこまでも続いてゆく広がりをもっている。

アルティガスの住宅における子供室の考え方は，生きている空間を感じさせる部分である。自邸(1960年)では，子供が成長する段階で彼等の領域を完全に切り離して木立ちの奥に建てた。この住宅では，子供の領域を示す装置として独立したパティオを与えている。こうした細やかな部分に，シンプルな架構とは似ても似つかないデリケートな気遣いが見られる。

この住宅へのアプローチの楽しさは，私にとって忘れられないものの一つである。それは，緩やかな階段を右手に上がると，家族全員がプールで泳いでいたといった光景であり，住宅へのアプローチとして実に印象に残るものだ。　　　　(鈴木恂)

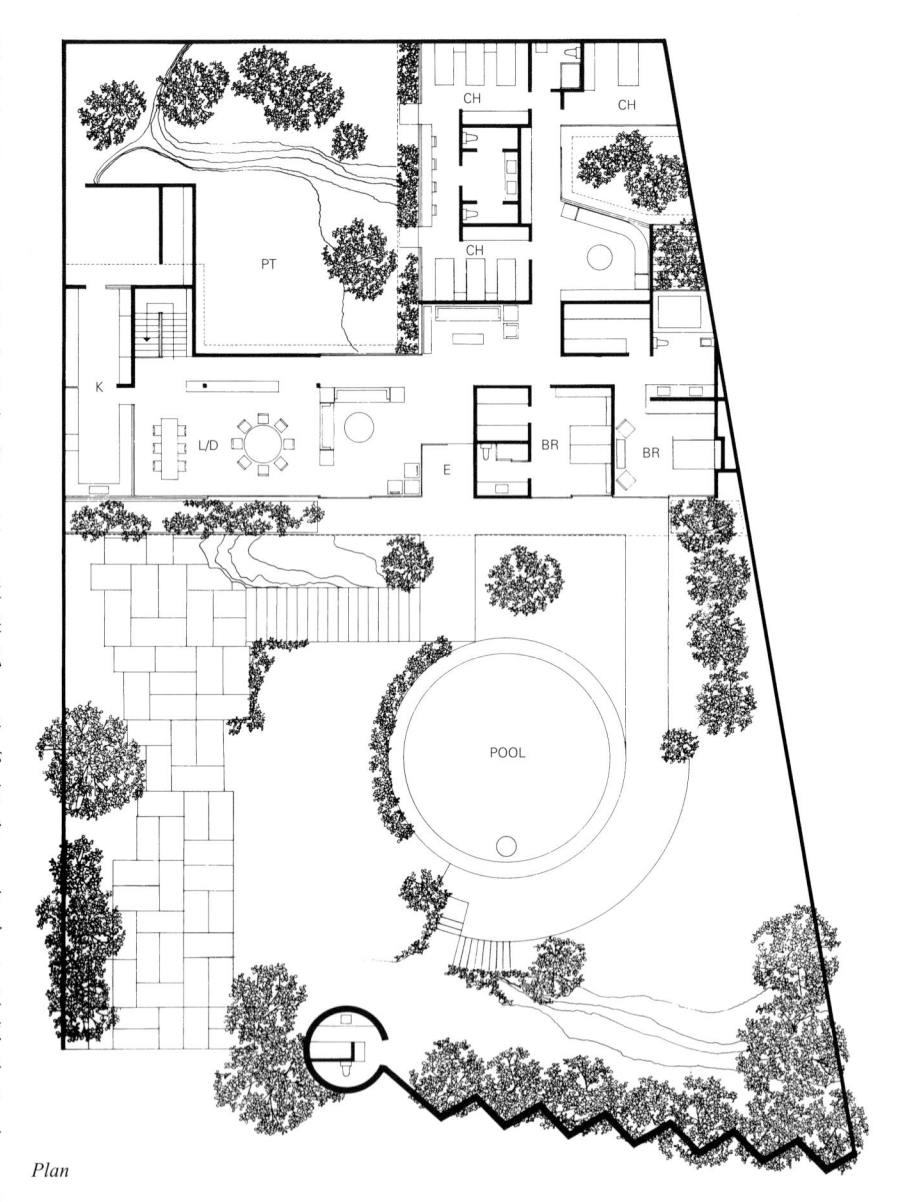

Plan

Veiw from approach アプローチより見る

Pool プール

Approcah: stairs leading to entrance (right)　アプローチ：玄関への階段（右）

Living room on left, approach and pool on right　左は居間，右がアプローチとプール

Living room: looking patio 居間：中庭を見る

Powder room (left) and bedroom (right) 化粧室（左）と寝室（右）

Francisco Artigas & Fernando Luna House in San Angel

Mexico City, Mexico, 1966

Living room (left) and bedroom (right): looking entrance 居間（左）と寝室（右）：玄関を見る

Plan

View toward pool from living room　居間よりプールを見る

A 45 m x 25 m site is comparatively small in the Pedregal housing area. This house is laid diagonally, seemingly cutting into the sloping strip site.

The laying corner to corner and the extension of the interior spaces made possible by this rotation within the strict site boundaries is the most significant feature of this house. More precisely the quality of the space is characterized by various sized patios sandwiched within strong diagonal lines which serve as an axis and a 50 m main line of access.

In this project Artigas added another meaning to patio space—which is traditional. Each room has a patio, they vary in size and have different purposes. They not only take the role of providing the main general light source but also work as an aperture which takes in the more unique elements of the local day light characteristics, and these patios give us the impression that our sight is opened up.

Another characteristic of this house is the position of the bedroom and the suggested use of it. This bedroom is at a higher level than the outside living room (patio) and is thought of as a place from which to view the living room and the pool. This idea, having different kinds of living rooms, changes the relationship of inside and outside. This house was built in 1966, and when we look at the ardor given to Colonial style later, I can't help thinking that this house seems to be a turning point.

The meaning of the patios is expanded by the fluidity of the interior and exterior space—for the larger and smaller patios—and by the character of each room—for the third patio. The living room in the middle of the patio is thought of as an integral part of the patio, as is the pool. He repeats this arrangement with the patio as the living room in his own house (1960) which does not have a living room. He perceives the living room as the outside.
Makoto Suzuki

45メートル×25メートルというのは，ペドレガル住宅区にあっては小型の敷地である。細長くやや傾斜した敷地をダイアゴナルに切るように，この住宅は配置される。

この住宅の最大の特徴はこの対角の配置であり，対角軸によって振られた内部空間の伸びと歪みである。さらに細かくいうならば，軸線になっているサービスと長さ50メートルに及ぶ主動線に挟まれた，大小の中庭が決定づけている空間の質であるといえよう。

アルティガスの作品では，伝統的ともいえるパティオ・スペースは別の意味が加えられる。この住宅でもパティオは様々な目的と規模で各個室に取りついている。それらは，光のコアとしての役割を果たすだけでなく，各部屋に独特な光を取り入れる装置でもあり，視界が開けた感じのするパティオでもある。

ここで取られている特徴のもう一つは，寝室の位置とその使い方に対する提案である。屋外としての居間（パティオ）よりも高い位置に置かれた寝室は，徹底して居間やプールを眺める場として考えられている。別の種類の居間をそこに組み入れることで，内と外の関係を微妙に変化させることにもなる。この住宅は1966年に建てられたが，その後の彼の作品に多く現れるコロニアルへの傾倒を考えるとき，この家はちょうどその分岐点にあるように思えてならない。

二つの大小のパティオは，全体を貫ぬく内外空間の流動によって，三つのパティオは個室の性格によって決められているように，中庭の意味は拡張されていく。パティオの中間に置かれた居間は，半屋内的なプール室と共にパティオの一部を構成していると考えられる。居間のない自邸（1960年）では，中庭を居間として模しているように，この住宅でも居間というアクティビティを屋外に近付けて捉えている。

（鈴木恂）

View toward living room from pool　プールより居間を見る

Living room　居間

Bedroom 寝室

Powder room: bedroom on left 化粧室：左は寝室

Francisco Artigas Architect's House

Mexico City, Mexico, 1960

View from patio 中庭より見る

Approach アプローチ

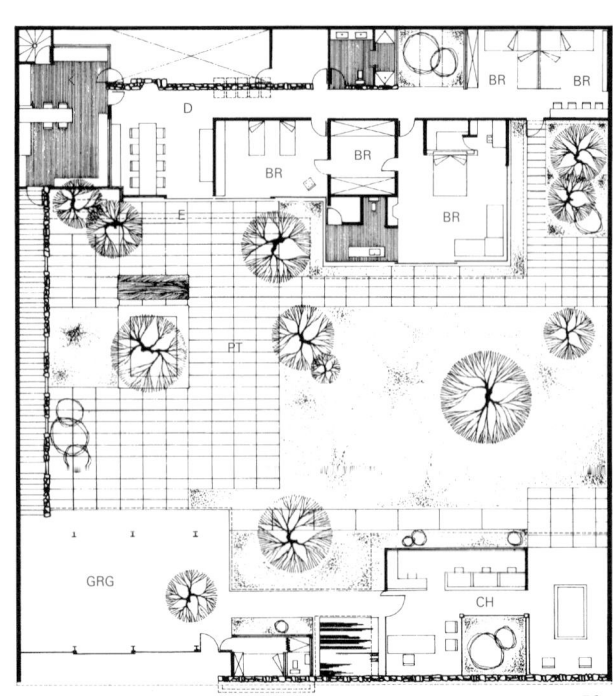

Plan

Living room 居間

House projects occupy an important position in Mexican modern architecture, endowed with enormous contributions from architects such as Barragán and Artigas. Barragán was responsible for the original idea and total planning of the residential district Pedregal in Mexico City, as well as for the production of the monument at the gate of this district. In turn, Artigas is the true builder, who has actually put into practice a design that heightened the standards of the housing district.

This house, the architect's own private residence, is located inside Obregon Park in the vicinity of university campus and Pedregal residential district. The site's thick grove of tall trees is an integral part of the park. Despite the site's vast extent and abundance of greenery, Artigas has chosen to give his own home a modest scale. One of his earlier works, this house is small in size but filled with challenges—a sort of his own case study, an experimental house. For instance, there is no living room in this house. The part called living room is in fact a dining room. This certainly is an attempt of pushing the living room outdoors, or merging it into the bedroom as a private space. The dining room and the bedrooms associate outdoor life with indoor life to such a point that they become indistinctive. Lunch table under the trees captures the living space's natural jump out in the open-air. The toplight over the bed that opens and shuts manually and an open arrangement of the toilet are excellent devices of endless pursuit of nature. And yet, there also is an interesting manipulation of effects of light from outside such as the miniature patio or the layout of the hallway in the back with respect to the garden.

Another distinctive feature in this house is the children's room which expanded itself according to the children's growth and later enlarged to twice the original floor area. It is interesting in the sense that this change seems to be progressing toward the formation of a patio surrounded by private spaces, that is, the invisible living room. After all, many houses in Pedregal residential district may be considered as consequences of his early ideas.
Makoto Suzuki

メキシコ現代建築において住宅作品が占める位置は大きい。その中でもバラガンやアルティガスの果した役割は非常に大きい。バラガンはメキシコ・シティの住宅区ペドレガルの企画者であり全体計画の立案者である。同時にそのゲートにあるモニュメントの制作者である。一方アルティガスはこの住宅地の本当の建設者で，住宅区の質的水準を高めた設計の実践者ということができる。

このアルティガスの自邸は大学都市とペドレガル住宅区に近いオブレゴン公園の中にある。セイバの大樹が繁る敷地は公園の一部を成している。この広さと緑の只中で彼自身の住宅は非常につつましいスケールでまとめられた。アルティガスの初期の作品であるこの自邸は規模としては小さいが，そこで試みられていることの数は多い。つまり彼のスタディであり実験住宅といえるものである。この住宅には居間がない。居間と呼ばれる部分は食堂である。ここで居間を屋外に追い出すこと，または個室としての寝室に吸収することを狙っているようだ。食堂も寝室も外の生活と内の生活を区別できないまでに結びつく。木影にあるランチ・テーブルなどは実に自然に飛び出して来たリビングの部分を捉えている。開閉の自由なベッドの上のトップライトや，トイレのオープンな配置は，自然の中に居てなお自然を求めようとする見事な装置といえる。それでいて背後の廊下と庭の取り方にも見られるように，坪庭のような外光の効果を生かしているところがおもしろい。

この住宅でもう一つの特徴は子供室である。子供が成長するに従って向い側の子供室部分が拡張され，後にこの平面の2倍程度に増築された。このことは見えない居間，すなわち，個室に囲まれたパティオを連想させる配置に近づいているようで興味深い。いずれにせよ，ペドレガル住宅区の多くの家は，こうした彼の初期のアイディアの結果と見ることができる。　　　　　（鈴木恂）

Corridor to bedroom　寝室へ至る廊下

Children's room wing: living room　子供室棟：居間

Bedroom　寝室

Approach to children's room　子供室へ至るアプローチ

Indoor pool　室内プール

Fernando Artigas
LAR/Fernando Romero

Virreyes House
Lomas de Chapultepec, Mexico, 1952*

*originally designed by F. Artigas and renovated by F. Romero in 2006

View from street on south　南側道路より見る

Approach　アプローチ

View from garden　庭より見る

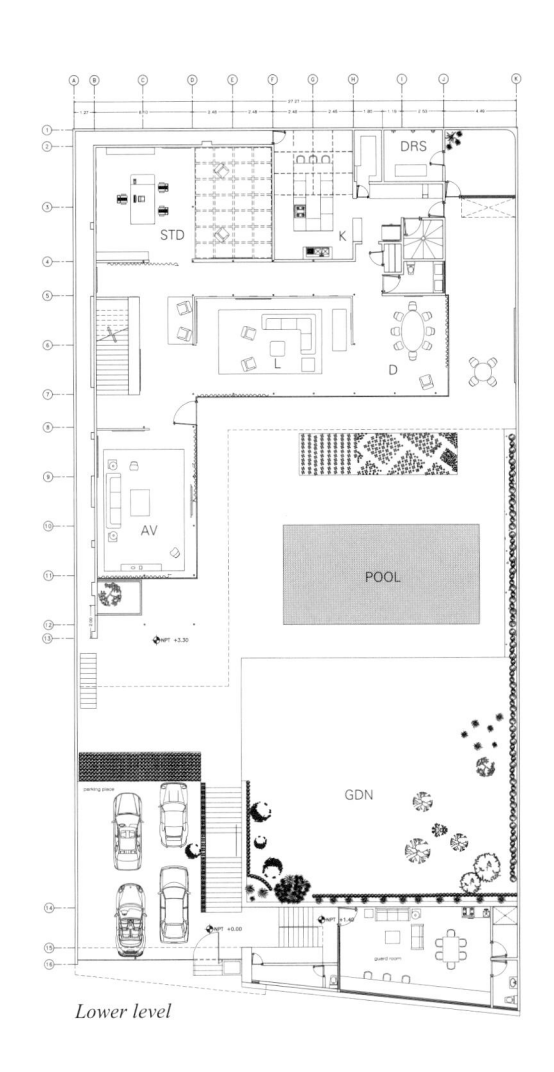

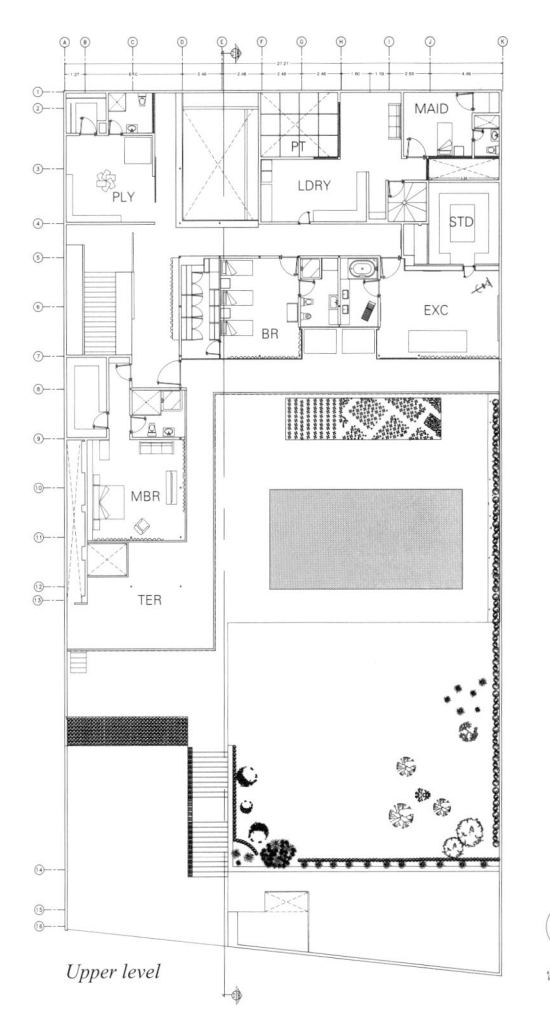

Lower level

Upper level

95

The house is located in Lomas de Chapultepec. This building dating from the fifties was designed by a renowned Mexican architect named Francisco Artigas.

Prior to the occupation of our client, the house had been used as a showroom for kitchens and furniture, with their respective administrative offices. These tenants had conditioned the property by adding some divisive walls made of frosted glass, which did not correspond to the original draft.

Access from the avenue is at one level below the house as well as the parking place with a capacity of six cars, utility room and security area. It is through a staircase made based compound (colored black volcanic stone) which is accessible to the garden and the ground floor of the house. The project is resolved in a scheme in the form of "L" and has two main levels.

On the ground floor public areas are integrated as lobby, TV room, living room, dining room, study and a covered terrace, as well as service areas such as the kitchen and service corridor that connects directly to the garage. The project is opened towards an extensive garden and a reflecting pond, which make up the visual points from the indoor areas. It has large windows that allow preserve privacy through the curtains that were added and chosen to combine with the original materials and furniture in the house.

The marble floor has shades of beige with brown streaks; large rugs were added to enable a greater degree of warmth in the areas such as living and TV room. The original project had screens attached to the metal structure of tubular columns, prepared from black granite, which were restored, polished and cleaned.

There is a double-height interior patio covered by a skylight that gives natural lighting to both stories, the floor of this patio is covered with black granite and one of its walls with granite "fly wing" in shades of gray. The purpose of changing materials achieves to emphasize this area, making it the focal point of the interior life.

The kitchen has "arabescato" marble paneling, which were restored, and in order to respect them as much as possible, the design of the kitchen was resolved through a central island, leaving the smooth walls to appreciate the gray streaks that this type of marble possesses.

In the upper floor, are the private areas conformed by bedrooms, gym, and their respective bathrooms, as well as peripheral terrace deck that becomes towards the lines of vision of the garden.

Living room　居間

View from living room toward garden　居間より庭を見る

Living room 居間△▽

この住宅は，高級住宅地，ロマス・デ・チャプルテペック地区に建っている。名高いメキシコ人建築家フランシスコ・アルティガスによって，1950年代に設計された。

施主の入居以前，この住宅は，個別の事務室がある，キッチンと家具のショールームとして使用されていた。このようなテナントによって，この建築は，オリジナルの図面には対応していない磨りガラスの区分壁が付加された状態となっていた。

通りからの入口は，6台分の駐車場やユーティリティ・ルームやセキュリティ・エリアと同様に，下階にある。入口は，着色された黒い火山石の合成材でできた階段へと続いていて，その階段は，庭と住宅の地上階へと通じている。このプロジェクトは，「L」字型の計画に解を求め，基本的に2階建てである。

地上階には，ロビー，TVルーム，リビング・ルーム，ダイニング・ルーム，書斎，屋根付きテラスといったパブリック・エリアがまとめられていて，他にも，ガレージに直結しているサービス用の廊下や，キッチンといった，サービス・エリアがある。この建築は，屋内エリアからの視覚的な特徴を作り出している広い庭と影を映しこむ池に面して，開かれている。また，室内のオリジナルの素材と家具とに一体化するように選ばれて，加えられたカーテンによって，プライバシーを保つことのできる大きな窓がある。

大理石の床は，ベージュに茶色の筋が入った色合いで，リビング・ルームやTVルームといったエリアが大幅に温かくなるように，大きなラグが加えられた。オリジナルの計画では，黒い御影石で作られたスクリーンが，チューブ状の柱の金属構造部分に取り付けられていた。このスクリーンは，修復され，磨かれて，洗いをかけられた。

スカイライトに覆われた，2層吹き抜けの屋内パティオがあり，両方の階に自然光が降り注いでいる。このパティオの床は，黒い御影石が敷き詰められ，壁の一つには，「空を飛ぶ翼」のような模様のグレーの色合いをした御影石が使われている。素材を変化させたことによって，このエリアが屋内生活の中心となるよう，強調されるのである。

キッチンは，修復された「アラベスカート」という名の色合いをした大理石で羽目板張りになっている。これらの大理石の羽目板を可能な限り重んじるために，キッチンの設計はアイランド型として，このタイプの大理石が有するグレーの筋を鑑賞するために，なめらかな壁面をそのままにしている。

上階には，寝室，ジム，それぞれ個別の浴室，また，庭に向かった視覚的なラインとなる外周のテラスによって，プライベート・エリアが構成されている。

Jaime Ortiz Monasterio Obregon House
Mexico City, Mexico, 1960s

Night view over pool プール越しの夜景

The tendency of contemporary architecture in Mexico changed dramatically approaching 1965. We could easily consider this tendency as simply being a reaction to the trends which had been accumulated through the 1950's. However it seems to be more likely that this was also the result of the stimulation which was given to the younger generation by the freedom they received from breaking with the colonial style. However we cannot completely explain this serious breakaway from the style of the revolution era only with this. It is clear that other social movements such as those found in the architecture of northern America whose influence was growing, and the standardization or prefabrication which was brought inevitably by the nation's industrialization, had a significant effect on the architecture of Mexico as well.

The first criticism of these design tendencies was the disregarding of the climate. The second came from the feeling that it was a simple copying or importing of foreign (American) culture. At this time, problems caused by the hot climate were not adequately resolved, even in the houses designed by J. O. Monasterio who employed experimental glazing a lot, Manuel Gonzalez Rul, Ramón Torres. I should point out that Mexico was the first Latin American country to use glass curtain walls extensively and no other neighboring countries followed.

The Obregon House is rather a collection of parts of a house. The parts this house contains are a guest room, study and private gallery only. This house is segregated from the main dwelling by a 4 m high stone wall. However they share a generous garden and pond. A one-piece HP shell roof and four glass walls became possible only because of the limited functions inside.
Makoto Suzuki

1965年を境にして，メキシコにおける現代建築の傾向が大きく変わる。50年代を通して築きあげたものへの反抗としてその傾向を受けとめられなくはないが，コロニアル様式と訣別したことによって得られた自由な方法の時代が，若いジェネレーションに与えた刺激であると見た方がよい。ただ，民族の伝統を戦旗に抱いて戦った時代との大きな断絶が，それだけでは説明出来ないことは確かだ。影響力を大きくしていく北米建築の動向，国が工業化されることで必然的にもたらされる規格化やプレファブ化，こうした社会的変動が建築に深く関わるのは当然のことである。

このような傾向に対してなされた多くの非難の一つは気候風土の無視についてであった。また，アメリカへの迎合と追随に対する憤りに似た感情からくる非難もあった。この時代，ガラスを多用して次々に実験的な住宅を建てたJ・モナステリオ，M・ゴンザレス・ルー，R・トレスといった人々の作品においても，気候や熱い風土の問題を充分には解決していない。中南米の住宅でガラスのカーテンウォールをここまで極端に使用したのは，メキシコが最初であり他国に類を見ないことも指摘しておこう。

オブレゴン邸は住宅というより住宅の一部である。隣接する主住居部分とは，4メートル程度の高さをもつ石塀で隔離され独立している。ただ広大な庭や池は共通の部分である。HPシェルの一枚の屋根と四周のガラスは，限定された内部機能から初めて成立し得たものである。　　　　（鈴木恂）

Patio with sculpture　彫刻のあるパティオ

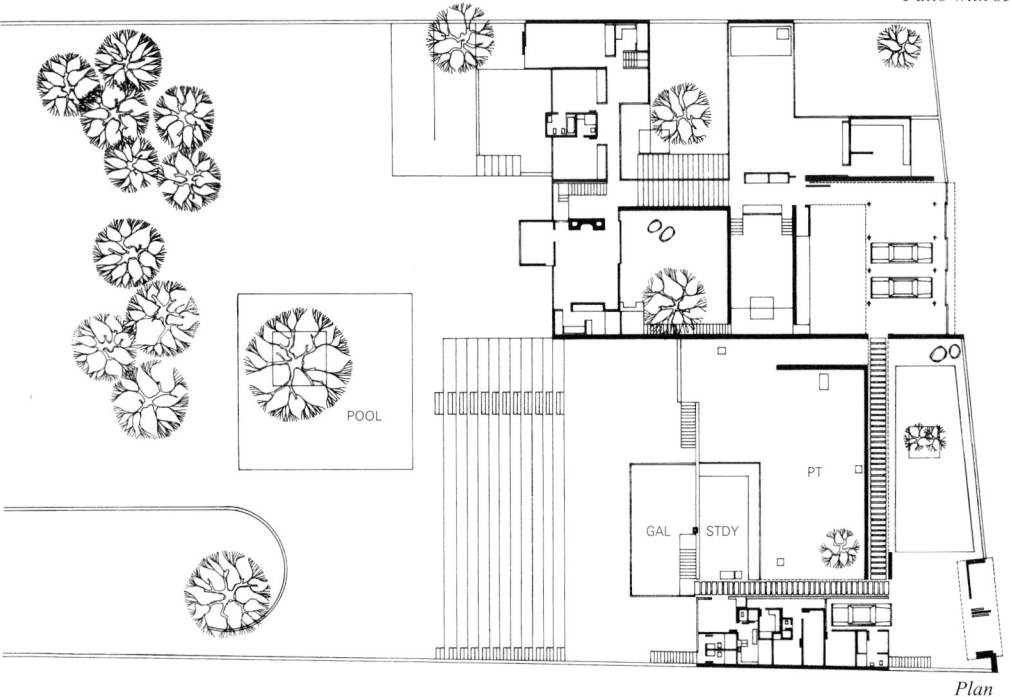

Plan

Living room 居間

Living room on left, study on right　左に居間，右に書斎

Study on upper level　上階にある書斎

Contemporary Mexican Houses after Barragán
Miquel Adria

バラガン後のメキシコ現代住宅
ミケール・アドリア

The contemporary house is one of the most fertile laboratories of recent Mexican architecture. As original element and inhabitable object, the house is both a manifesto and a summing up of intentions. It is through the house—through their own houses, in some cases—that architects define their positions. The house becomes a demonstration of the architect's attitude to place, to the dichotomy between tradition and modernity.

The Mexican house is large and unique. It never explores standardized or repeatable solutions. It rejects neither the spatial advantages of tradition nor the comforts of modernity. Some Mexican houses draw on the sobriety of the vernacular tradition, the breadth of its spaces and its emphasis on privacy, to open from within onto the home as perfect refuge. They turn to account the ambiguous relationship between exterior and interior, a mastery of light, and in some cases a skillful handling of color. Others explore the potential of new technologies within the reach of local industry in carrying out formal exercises. But it would be difficult to speak of contemporary Mexican architecture without reference to the legacy of Barragán.

Luis Barragán (1902-88) earned a place as doubtless the most important Mexican architect of the twentieth century, inspiring successive generations with his passion for color and surfaces. His works are silent dialogues between blind walls and filtered light, the result of an act of syncretism between modernity and Mexican particularity. After Barragán, the preference for form, even when emptied of content, would remain a component of the various trends, with an emphasis on the closed rather than the open, the representative rather than the functional, and the aesthetic rather than the ethical.

The twentieth century ended with a range of different currents which offer a glimpse of the complexity and richness of contemporary architecture. The panorama extends from the solid, abstract work in chiseled concrete of González de León, through the patios enclosed by painted walls and the metaphysical towers of Legorreta, to the reincorporation of international styles by TEN Arquitectos. González de León (1926-) combined concrete brise-soleils, organic forms, and rough, exposed finishes—part of the legacy he received from Le Corbusier—with Pre-hispanic elements such as mounds, ramps, and broad stairways. Ricardo Legorreta (1931-) learned directly from Barragán and became the principal exporter of the smooth surfaces, blank walls, and vivid colors of a typically "Mexican" architecture. And Enrique Norten (1954-), along with others of his generation, has opened up not only new architectural frontiers, but a new panorama of formal and stylistic resources.

The house González de León built for himself in the Condesa neighborhood of Mexico City is at once a manifesto and an architectural self-portrait. In it can be found all of the canonic elements of his oeuvre, with its grouping of volumes, rotations, cubes, cylinders, brise-soleils, taluses,

現代住宅は，近年のメキシコ建築において，最も実り多く創造性に富んだ実験場の一つである。住宅は始原的なものとして，かつ居住できるオブジェとしてマニフェストであり，またあらゆる試みの総体なのだ。建築家は住宅を通し，それは時に自邸でもあるのだが，自らの立場を示す。つまり住宅は，場所性または近代と伝統という二面性に対する建築家の意識を体現している。

メキシコの住宅は大きくかつユニークである。規格化，または使い古されたデザインは一切なく，かといって伝統建築の持つ優れた空間性や近代的な快適さを否定もしない。家によっては土着の伝統建築の持つ慎ましさを基に作られ，空間の広がりやプライバシーを重視し，住宅を完全に保護された空間として，その内において開放的なものとしている。それらの住宅が重きを置くのは，外と内の移ろいゆく関係性や，光に対する深い理解，また時に卓越された色使いである。その一方，形態試行を繰り返しながら，地域の産業が許す限りにおいて，新しい技術の可能性を探求している住宅も存在する。しかしながら，バラガンが残したものの抜きにメキシコにおける現代住宅を語る事は難しいだろう。

ルイス・バラガン（1902-88年）は，間違いなく20世紀における最も重要なメキシコ人建築家であり，色や表面に対する自身の強い思いで，彼に続く世代の建築家に多大な影響を及ぼした。彼の建築は，窓のない壁と間接光による静かなる対話である。それは，モダニティとメキシコ土着の特異性の融合から生まれたものであった。バラガン後も，フォルムに対する美意識は，それらの全てが内実を伴っているわけではないが，様々なトレンドの一部となり継承されている。それらは，開放的であるよりも閉鎖的であることに，機能的であるよりも表現的であることに，また論理的であるよりもむしろ美的である事に重きを置く。

20世紀の終わりに際し，メキシコには様々な建築の潮流が生まれ，その中に現代建築の持つ複雑さや奥深さといったものを垣間見ることができた。この建築的パノラマは広範囲に渡り，ゴンザレス・デ・レオン（1926年〜）による研ぎ出しコンクリートを用いた量感のある抽象的な作品，レゴレッタのペイントされた壁に囲まれたパティオや形而上的な塔，さらにTENアルキテクトスによるインターナショナルスタイルの再解釈にまで及ぶ。ゴンザレス・デ・レオンは，コンクリートのブリーズ・ソレイユ，有機的なフォルム，さらにコルビジエの影響の一つである荒々しい打放し面などを，マウンドやスロープ，また大階段といった植民地時代以前から存在した建築言語と組み合わせた。バラガンから直に学んだリカルド・レゴレッタ（1931年〜）は，滑らかな表面，無装飾の壁，「メキシコ的」建築の代名詞である鮮やかな色，といった要素の一番の継承者となった。エンリケ・ノルテン（1954年〜）は同世代の建築家と共に，新しい建築の領域に足を踏み入れただけではなく，新たな形態および様式を内包する建築的パノラマを展開した。

ゴンザレス・デ・レオンがメキシコシティのコンデサ地区に建てた自邸は，建築家としてのマニフェストであり彼自身のポートレートでもある。そこには彼の建築を特徴づけている要素が集約されているのだ。それらは，グループ化された

white concrete, and the three primary colors on the front door. Behind the blind facade of one side of its L-shaped plan are the parking areas, the services, and the master bedroom, which opens onto an interior patio. The other wing, perpendicular to the street, contains the social areas of living room, dining room, and the architect's extraordinary library. A study closes out the domestic program around a paved patio, with a swimming lane and a sloping mound of grass. González de León's work as a painter and sculptor—performed to the sound of Baroque arias and contemporary symphonies—is reflected in the proportions of every domestic element, in the truncated vaults and the pergolas that integrate the construction with its neighbors.

Ricardo Legorreta has constructed a spectacular collection of singular houses which began with the 'Montalbán Residence' in Los Angeles and are now scattered throughout Mexico, the United States, Israel, and Japan. Attentive to the conditions of the site, to climate and topography, and to the needs of each client, he endows each of his houses with a character of its own, though certain constants give a very special identity to his work: patios, porticoes, and spaciousness. Particularly noteworthy are the house in California and the 'Laviada House' in the Lomas de Chapultepec neighborhood of Mexico City. The former reconciles the colonial typology of rooms facing onto a central patio with views of vineyards covering the rolling hills that surround the house. In the latter, a diagonal sequence of patios articulates a movement from the more public areas to the more private ones, generating richly ambivalent spaces on the line between interior and exterior.

The houses designed by Enrique Norten (TEN Arquitectos) are yet another proof of the conceptual clarity of his work. At the risk of sounding obvious, it might be said that his residences are effective diagrams of function and forceful responses to the needs of each user. Whereas the House LE projects a practically blind facade but opens up onto a longitudinal patio—demonstrating its effectiveness in contradiction of all logic—, the 'House AZ' and 'House R.R.' are resolved by means of efficient L-shaped plans. The stairways that join the different levels supply just the right vertical element. The striking facades and diaphanous spaces partake of the globalizing trends of contemporary architecture.

Alberto Kalach (1960-) takes the solidity of concrete masses from González de León, the use of intimate, angled lighting from Barragán, and a taste for large glass planes from Norten to create a hybrid but personal style. The 'GGG House' in the Chapultepec Golf Club development in Mexico City can be seen as the simplest and at the same time the richest and most complex of architectural expressions. Its spatial conception, inspired by the work of sculptor Jorge Yazpik, starts from a very basic distribution of the program and goes on to explore possibilities of form and spatial organization more freely through the use of clay maquettes.

ヴォリュームや，ローテーション（回転），立方体，円柱，ブリーズ・ソレイユ，岩でできたマウンド，白いコンクリート，そして正面扉に使われている3原色である。この住宅はL字型の平面を持ち，その一方に建つ窓の無いファサードの後ろ側には，ガレージ，設備スペース，そして内側のパティオに向けて開かれる主寝室が配置されている。通りと直角に建つもう片方のウイングは，リビング・ルームやダイニング・ルーム，また蔵書が極めて豊富な自身のライブラリーなどの社交的空間を内包する。書斎はパティオを囲む居住空間からは独立しており，プールや芝生で覆われたマウンドによって周りから遮断されている。画家であり彫刻家でもあるゴンザレス・デ・レオンの，バロック・アリアや現代交響曲のようにつくり上げられた作品は，住宅のあらゆる要素に反映されている。それら要素とは頂部を平らにしたアーチやパーゴラであり，それらが住宅と周囲を結び付けている。

リカルド・レゴレッタは，ロサンジェルスの「モンタルバン邸」を初めとして，現在ではメキシコ，アメリカ，イスラエル，さらには日本にも極めて良質な住宅を生み出している。敷地，気候や地形，さらにクライアントの要望を注意深く読み込み，それぞれの作品に独自の特徴をもたらしている。その一方，パティオ，ポルティコ，広がりのある空間といった，作品群に一貫して見られる要素は，彼の建物に特別なアイデンティティも与えている。特筆すべきは，このカリフォルニアに建つ住宅と，メキシコシティのロマス・デ・チャプルテペック地区に位置する「ラヴィアダ邸」である。前者は主要なパティオに沿って部屋を配置するというコロニアル建築的手法と，周りに広がる丘陵地を覆うブドウ畑の眺望とを融和させている。後者においては，斜め方向に配列されたパティオが，パブリックな空間からよりプライベートな空間への移行にリズムを与えており，内と外の境界線上に味わい深い融和的な空間を創出している。

エンリケ・ノルテン（TENアルキテクトス）による住宅もまた，彼の概念的な明瞭さを体現している。解りきった事を言うようであるが，彼の作る住宅は，機能と使い手の要望に対する徹底的な配慮が描くダイアグラム，と言えるかもしれない。「ハウスLE」は，実質的に窓の無いファサードを持つが，同時に縦長のパティオに開かれており，あらゆるロジックに相反しながらも有効な解を導き出している。その一方，「ハウスAZ」と「ハウスR.R.」は，無駄の無いL字型のプランで構成されている。それぞれのフロアを結ぶ階段室が垂直な要素として程よく配置されている。その印象的なファサードと，繊細で透明感のある空間は，現代建築のグローバルな潮流とも通じている。

アルベルト・カラチ（1960年〜）は，ゴンザレス・デ・レオンが作るコンクリートの量塊，バラガンの柔和な間接光の使い方，ノルテンが好んで使う大きなガラス面などを取り込んだハイブリッドな，それでいて独自の建築スタイルを築いている。メキシコシティのチャプルテペック・ゴルフクラブ開発地区に建つ「GGGハウス」は，非常にシンプルで，かつ際立って濃密で複雑な建築表現を持つ。こ

House in San Angel by González de León
ゴンザレス・デ・レオン設計，サン・アンヘルの住宅（元，自邸）

Each incision cut into the mass suggests new interventions that combine to form a volumetric whole. The house emerges from a great concrete monolith that is progressively fragmented within a spatial grid defined by the gradual merging of a sphere into a cube and vice versa. The user moves through a sequence of shadows, bright light, and penumbra which contrast the spaces and mark the passage of time. Gardens, pools, patios, pavilions, and alcoves are connected through the grooves that break up the monolith in different directions.

Not long afterwards, Kalach designed the 'Bross House' in brick and concrete along one of the ravines that cut across the western outskirts of Mexico City. Unlike its neighbors, which face onto the street, this house moves away to enjoy the coolness of the ravine. A tower contains the library and the staircase, with living areas set among gardens on either side. A ramp leads from the garden to the rooftop and the bedroom; the kitchen, in the center of the house, is illuminated by a skylight; a pool reflects the sky and gathers rainwater, running it off into a cistern underneath the secret garden.

Kalach's work is perhaps the most original and sculptural. His buildings are radical responses, devised from the geometry of his plans and the incisions in his walls, which filter light into the interior spaces.

After forming part of TEN Arquitectos for more than ten years, Bernardo Gómez-Pimienta began a solo career with his own house in Valle de Bravo. It is an independent pavilion on the same lot as his family home. The new construction assumes the requirements and the restrictions of both the domestic program and the rural architecture that prevails in the zone. A roof sloping in contrary direction covers a diaphanous glass box which contains the living areas and the master bedroom. The stone base houses the children's bedrooms and storage areas. Everything in this paradigmatic house has been designed by the architect himself: railings, tables, armchairs, windows, and stainless steel columns. A swimming pool occupies the back patio between the house and the street.

A short time later Gómez-Pimienta built the 'House GDL' on the edge of Guadalajara. In this house, it is not what is included that counts, but what is left out. The superposition of two orthogonal prisms that reflect the division of private and public spaces generates a cruciform artifact out of which absences emerge. Thus, the center of the house becomes a void, and the few elements crossing it pursue immateriality from the transparency of the glazed footbridge; or the muscular metallic framework—which holds the upper parallelepiped in place—vanishes into the neutrality of its stone or glass walls. For Gómez-Pimienta, the orthogonal superimposition of the prisms conforms to an autonomous order, rather than to the place or the expression of their constructive logic. In this house, the most obvious column is the one that is not there, the central space is the one that is emptied out, and the most spectacular place is the

の住宅の空間概念は，ホルヘ・ヤスピクの彫刻からヒントを得ている。それはごく基本的なプログラムの配置に始まり，後に粘土の模型を用い，フォルムや空間構成の可能性をより自由に探る試みに至る。マッスに入れられた切込みは，各々が家全体を統合する役割を担っている。この住宅はコンクリートの巨大なヴォリュームから成り，そのヴォリュームは，徐々に球が立方体に，またはその逆のプロセスにより定義される空間グリッドの中で，漸進な断片化を見せる。使い手は，連続して立ち現れる影や明るい光，さらに空間を際立たせ，時間の移ろいを刻む影と光の境界部内を移動する。庭，池（プール），パティオ，パヴィリオン，アルコーブは，この巨大なヴォリュームを様々な方向へ分節する切込みによって繋がっている。

カラチは，「GGGハウス」の設計まもなく「ブロス邸」を設計した。それはコンクリートとレンガでできており，メキシコシティの西のはずれを切り裂く渓谷の一つに建っている。周辺の建物が通りに面して建っているのに対し，この住宅は渓谷の涼しさを堪能できるような配置となっている。塔に読書室と階段室があり，他の居室は庭に沿って置かれている。スロープが庭から屋上そして寝室へと繋がっており，住宅の中央に位置するキッチンは，トップライトからの光を受ける。池は空を映し出し，雨水を集め，あふれ出た水はシークレット・ガーデンの下に置かれた貯水槽に蓄えられる。

カラチの作品は，最も独創性に溢れ，彫刻的であると言えるだろう。彼の建築は，彼の平面幾何学と，光を室内へ通す壁に施された切り込みにより創造される，根源的な解の総体なのだ。

10年以上に及ぶTENアルキテクトスでの経験を経て，ベルナルド・ゴメス＝ピメンタはバイエ・デ・ブラボにある自邸の設計を機に独立した。これは，彼の家族の家と同じ敷地内に建つ離れである。この家は，必要とされるプログラムや周辺村落の建築からの影響をそのまま受け入れている。反対方向に勾配をとられた屋根は，居室や主寝室を含む半透明なガラスの箱を覆っている。石でできた台座部分には，子供部屋と納戸が配置されている。自身のパラダイム的存在であるこの家のあらゆるもの，手摺，テーブル，肘掛け椅子，窓，ステンレスの柱に至るまで建築家自身によってデザインされた。住宅と通りに挟まれた裏のパティオには，プールが設けられている。

自邸の設計後しばらくしてから，ゴメス＝ピメンタはグアダラハラの外れに建設された「ハウスGDL」を設計した。この住宅においては，何が存在するかではなく，何が不在かが重要である。プライベートな空間，そしてパブリックな空間としてそれぞれ機能する二つの積層されたガラスの直方体は，十字型の構造物となり空洞を作り出す。よって住宅の中心はヴォイドとなっており，そこを横断する幾つかの要素には非物質的な装いが求められた。それらは透明なガラスのブリッジ，上部の平行六面体を支える骨太なメタリック・フレームであり，それぞれ石やガラスの壁がもつ無機質さの中に溶け込んでいく。ゴメス＝ピメンタにとっ

one that cannot be crossed: the twelve-meter cantilever; the void that articulates the two superposed bodies; and the reflecting pool that separates the interior vestibule from the distant, alien landscape of formless Guadalajara. This house emphasizes the lightness and interior transparency of an apparently hermetic artifact.

Michel Rojkind (1969-) is one of several emerging architects who are making their voices heard on the local and international scene. Along with others such as Derek Dellekamp, Javier Sánchez, Central de Arquitectura, Mauricio Rocha, Fernando Romero, and Tatiana Bilbao, he is beginning to make a name for himself in some global forums. Rojkind is perhaps the most audacious, running greater formal risks and showing greater conceptual innovation. If some of Rojkind's designs have served mainly to try out new materials, his 'Pr House' is an exercise in formal gratification and the autonomy of the architectural object. The construction is an annex which crowns a residence built in the 1970s, with an autonomous program that removes the new apartment to the rooftop of the original house. A red Möbius strip of soldered steel frames the vistas of a program consisting of a living room on one side and a bedroom on the other. The treatment of the rooftop garden as a sort of lounge provides the antechamber to this domestic jewel on the sprawling hillsides of Tecamachalco.

All of these turn-of-the-new-century houses share a certain autobiographical character: they are personal works, they are architects' houses. Some of them conceive the house as a concatenation of spaces and patios; others move in quest of an ideal, Platonic space. Some are to live in; others are settings for social events. They cause the heroic architectures of the mid-twentieth century, which created some of the finest houses in the expanding metropolis of Mexico City, to linger in the memory, as well as the spatial richness and modernist-vernacular syncretism of Luis Barragán. And in their ambiguity between interior and exterior and their adept handling of space, all of these houses preserve a certain Mexican flavor.

て，ガラスの直方体の積み上げは，場所性や直方体という構築的ロジックの表現ではなく，あくまで彼自身の意図に従ったものである。この住宅においてとりわけ目を引く柱は，そこに不在のそれであり，中心の空間は，何も無い空洞で，際立って壮観な場所は，横断することが不可能な場所である。それらはそれぞれ，12メートルのキャンティレバー，積層する二つのヴォリュームを統合するヴォイド，住宅の玄関と遠方に広がる姿の捉えづらいグアダラハラの地形とを隔てるプールである。この住宅は，密閉された芸術作品のごとく，軽さや内部における透明度を強調している。

ミシェル・ルーキング（1969年〜）は，メキシコのみならず国際的にその存在を知られつつある若手建築家の一人である。デレク・デルカンプ，ハビエル・サンチェス，セントラル・デ・アルキテクチューラ，マウリシオ・ローシャ，フェルナンド・ロメロ，そしてタチアナ・ビルバオ等と共に，その名前は国際的フォーラムの場でも徐々に聞かれる存在となっている。ルーキングはその中でもとりわけ独創的で，果敢に新たなフォルムへの挑戦を図り，概念的な部分においてより大きな革新を試みている建築家と言えるだろう。仮に彼の作品の多くが，主に新しいマテリアルの可能性を探るものであるとしたら，「Rrハウス」は形態賛美，および建築物の持ちうる自立性に対する試みである。この家は，70年代に建てられた住宅の上部に増築されたアネックスであり，自立したプログラムとして既存の住宅の屋上に置かれた新しいペントハウスである。溶接されたスティールで構成される一続きの赤い帯は，一方のリビング・ルーム，もう一方の寝室というこの建物の外観を形成している。既存の屋上庭園をラウンジ的な場所とすることで，テカマチャルコに広がる丘陵地に光る宝石のようなこのペントハウスへのアプローチを演出している。

新世紀に際して生み出されたこれらの住宅は，それぞれに自伝的な特徴を帯びている。それらは個人的な作品であり，建築家の自邸である。住宅を空間とパティオのつながりとして捉えているものもあれば，より観念的でプラトニックな空間を追求したものもある。住まいもあれば，社交的なイベントの場となるものもある。これらの住宅は，ルイス・バラガンの空間的な濃密さ，および彼による近代性とメキシコ固有性との融合とともに，20世紀中頃，大都市として成長していたメキシコシティの中に，際立って良質な住宅をもたらしたヒロイックな建築群の遺伝子を受け継いでいる。全住宅を通し，それらが持つ内であり外であるという融和的な空間や，熟達された空間構成の中に，ある種のメキシコ的な趣を味わうことができる。

Legorreta Arquitectos House in Valle de Bravo
Valle de Bravo, Mexico, 1972–73

Main house: view from living room　母屋：居間からの眺め

Cottage and studio　コテージとスタジオ

Main House

The theme of this house was its integration with the landscape, informality and flexibility.

The roof built in the traditional style of the vernacular architecture of this area follows the slope of the hill at approximate 1.5 meters above ground, so the house is half sunken. As to the creation of three stories, the main elements of the house are composed of: a master bedroom, a living area and children's bedroom, which do not have furniture. The use of sleeping bags gives flexibility, not only of space but in the number of people who can sleep.

The exterior of the house is painted in the same color as that of the earth. There is no "designed" landscape. The local natural vegetation was developed and encouraged until it practically covers the house.

All the windows were designed from the inside according to views and light desired for the appropriate ambience of the room without any formal design study of the facade.

Cottage and Studio

Located at 500 meters from main house, there is a studio of the owner. It consists of only one room with a terrace.

Designed with the same philosophy as main house, it is intended to create a quiet and spiritual space where creativity is encouraged. Light, view and music are the basic complement of the architecture.

Walls were covered with mud in its natural color.

Main house: entry to terrace　母屋：テラス脇の入口

Terrace of main house　母屋のテラス

107

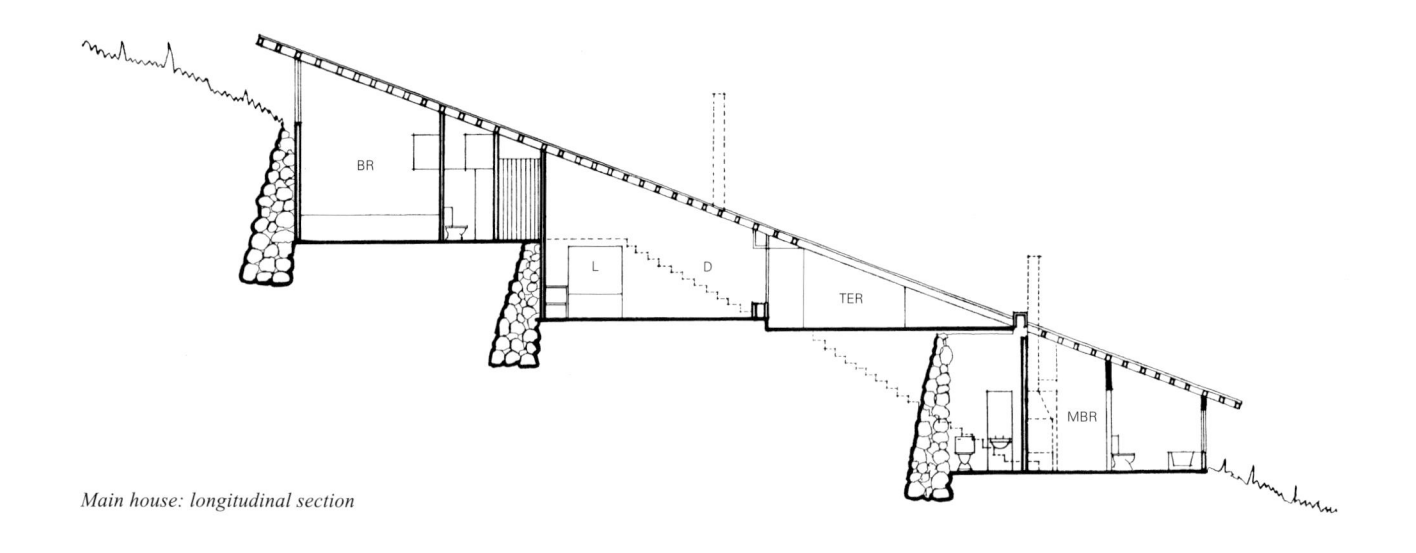

Main house: longitudinal section

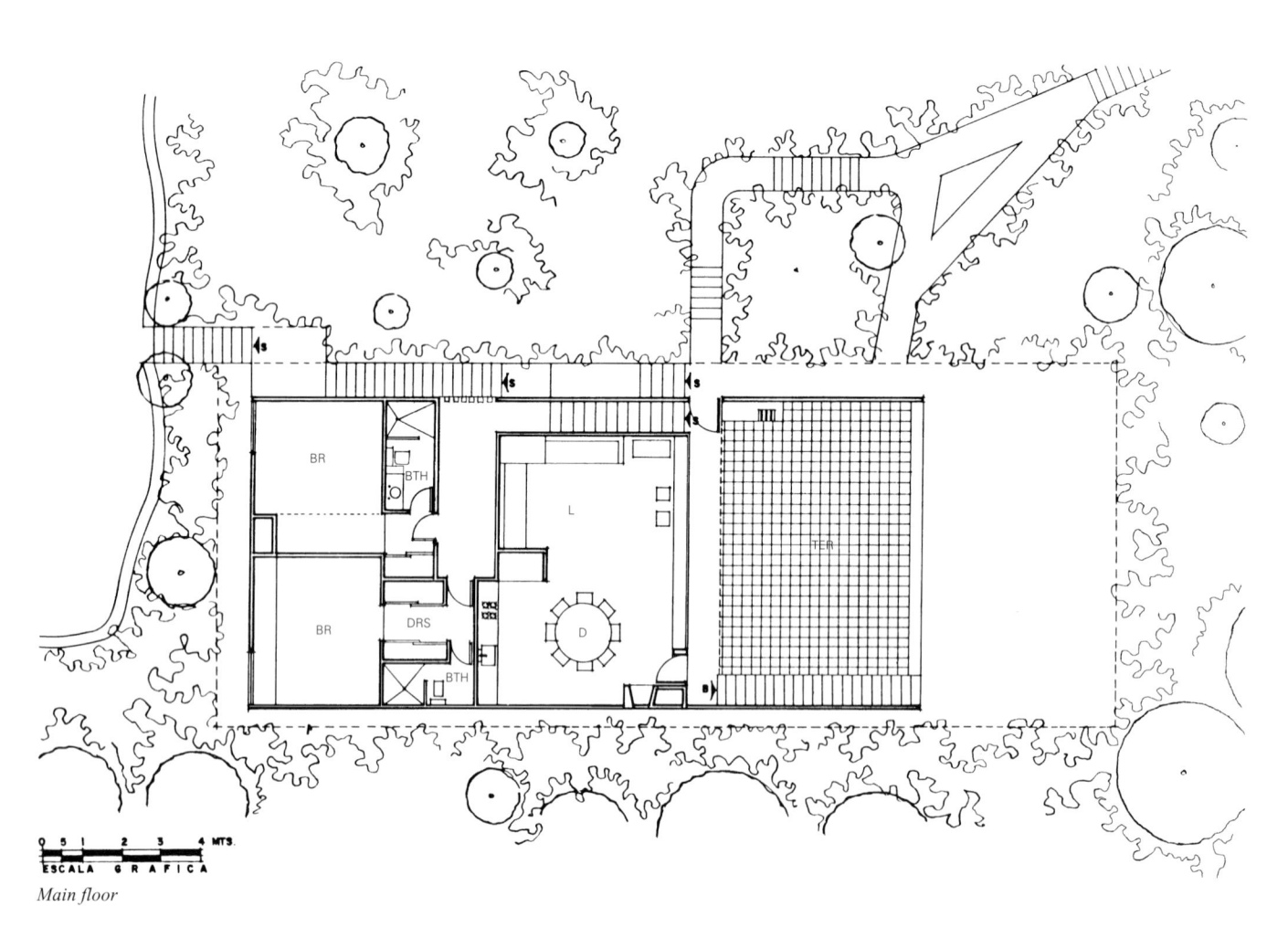

Main floor

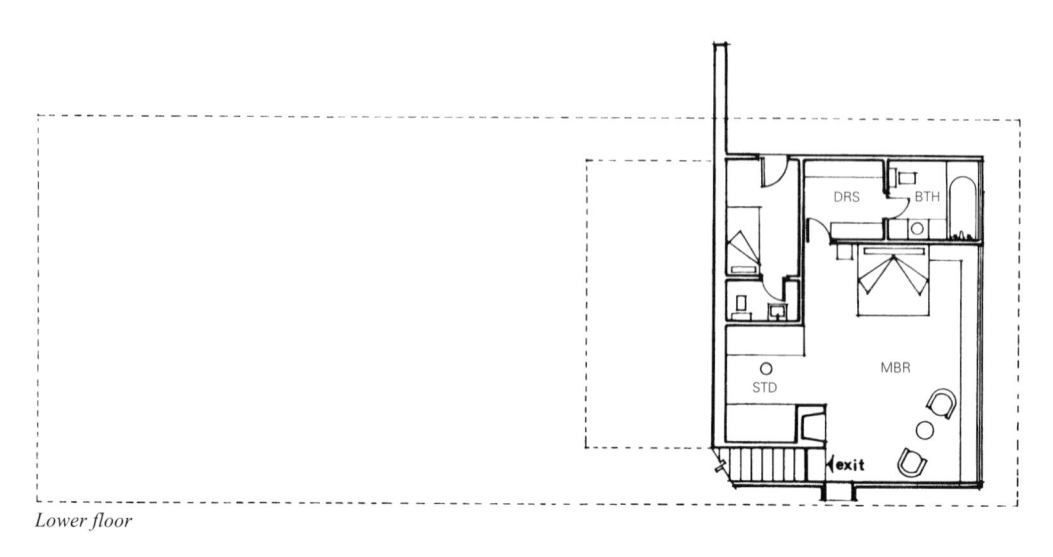

Lower floor

108

〈母家〉
　自然と一体化し，形式ばらず，フレキシブルな住宅を設計することがテーマであった。この地方に特有の建築様式を持つ屋根は，丘の斜面に沿って，地上1.5メートルほどの高さを保って延びているので，建物は半分地面に身を沈めた形になっている。3層から成り，主寝室，居間エリア，子供部屋がそれぞれを占めている。子供部屋にはベッドをおかず，寝袋を使うことにして空間にフレキシビリティをもたせたばかりでなく，大勢が泊まれるようにした。
　外壁には大地と同じ色を塗った。"人工的"なランドスケーピングは一切していない。この地方特有の植生が，やがて住宅を包みこむだろう。
　窓はすべて，ファサードの形態的スタディは何もせずに，各部屋の雰囲気にふさわしい眺めと光の入り具合を考えて，内側からデザインした。

〈コテージとスタジオ〉
　母屋から500メートル離れたところに建つ，施主のスタジオである。テラスと一部屋だけの構成である。
　母屋と同じ考え方で設計されているが，想像力が駆り立てられるような，静かで，精神的な空間となるように意図した。光，眺め，音楽が，この建物を完結させる。
　壁は泥で塗り込め，その自然な色合いを生かしている。

Studio スタジオ△▽

Living room on main floor　主階居間

Master bedroom on lower floor　下階主寝室

Living room of cottage　コテージの居間

Terrace of cottage　コテージのテラス

Legorreta Arquitectos   House in Southern California

Santa Fe, California, U.S.A., 1986–88

A magnificent site with a very ample program that called for an elegant house. In reality they are two houses that were to be separated but linked by some device, which eventually became a gallery.

The house was to be a second home but eventually it became the permanent residence for a highly successful businessman and his cultured wife. The design was intended to reflect the owner's personality: elegant, simple, human and peaceful.

My reaction was not to make a monument but to make a structure that blends into the landscape and could look like a wall at the top of the hill. Horizontality is the architectural theme.

Space and light are used to create the natural environment for excellent art pieces that are placed in a natural almost native way.

The climate and the family life style called for intensive outdoor living, so terraces, a swimming pool and a tennis court are located in a series of spaces that take advantage of light, shadow, color and water.

Fortunately the contractor's hobby is old wood, so the gallery and the main living spaces take advantage of old beams and significant doors are made of rough wood.

Each room was designed to have its own personality allowing the family to enjoy different experiences in each of them.

Views, light and color are controlled, so they are enjoyed in a mysterious way.

Finally landscape and furniture were designed to integrate with the architecture in such a way that they do not compete, but enhance the overall design.

洗練された住宅を必要とする，非常に広範なプログラムをもつ素晴らしい敷地。実際には分かれているが，ある方法──結局それはギャラリーとなった──で連絡している2棟の建物で構成されている。

この住宅はセカンドハウスになるはずだったが，最終的には，相当な成功をおさめた実業家と教養の高い夫人の常住の家となった。洗練され，質素で人間味のあるおだやかな人物というクライアントの人格を設計に反映させることを意図した。

モニュメントをつくるのではなく，風景の中に溶け込み，丘の頂きの壁のように見える建物をつくろうと思った。水平性が建築上のテーマである。

優れた美術品の数々を，そこにはじめからあったように，さりげなく飾るための，自然な環境が生まれるように空間と光を操作した。

この地の気候と家族の生活スタイルには，戸外での生活の場を充実させる必要があったので，テラス，水泳プール，テニスコートを光や陰，色彩，水を効果的に用いた空間の連なりの間に配置していった。

幸い，建設業者の趣味が古木材を集めることだったので，ギャラリーとメインの居間には古い木の梁を利用し，主要な扉には自然のままの木を使うことができた。

家族のひとりひとりが，独自の生活を楽しむことができるように，各個室はそれぞれの個性に合わせ変化をもたせた。

眺め，光，色彩をコントロールして，神秘的な雰囲気が楽しめるようにした。

風景と家具は，互いに張り合うことなく全体の効果を高めるように配慮し，建築と一体となるようにデザインされている。

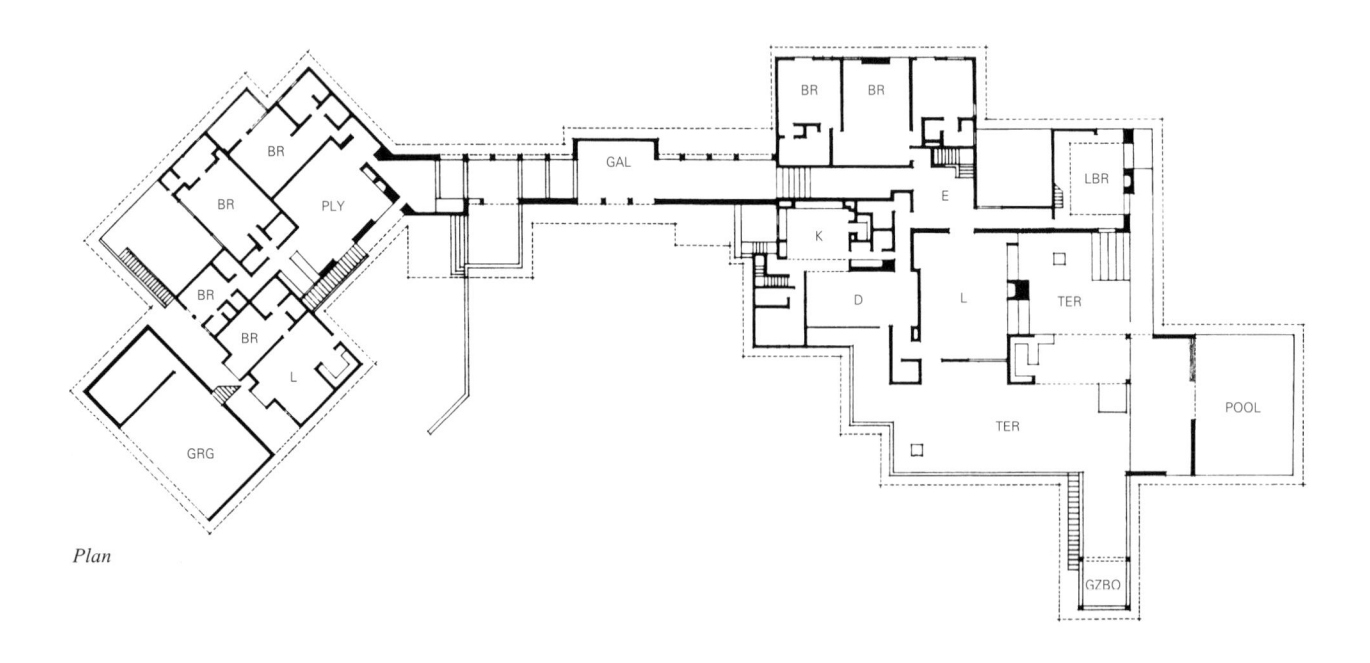

Plan

Distant view 遠景

Pool on right, gazebo on left 右にプール，左に東屋

Pool プール

View from pool toward terrace　プールよりテラスを見る

Entrance court　エントランス・コート

Library ライブラリー

Living room facing terrace テラスに面した居間

Gallery ギャラリー

Legorreta Arquitectos La Colorada House

Valle de Bravo, Mexico, 1994–95

Entrance patio　エントランス・パティオ△▷

Terrace テラス

Living room 居間

Located in a five acre site the house faces south to take advantage of views and sunlight.

It is intended to create intimacy, romanticism and privacy for the life of a family very active in business during the week and looking for rest and peace in the weekend.

The entrance and life style are conceived by continuous experiences of light, water and color, creating different atmospheres for the living and dining room, for the pool and for the bedrooms. The presence of views, courtyards and sky is continuous.

The roofs are wood beams with tile, plaster red walls and stone in the pool towers give the house unique personalities.

The architects design all the interiors including furniture, doors, knobs, accessories up to the last detail. They also designed the landscape.

5エーカーの敷地内の，眺めが良く日射しの注ぐ南向きに位置している。

週日は仕事に忙しく，週末はゆっくりと休みたいという一家のために，居心地良く，現実から離れ，プライバシーの守られた環境をつくり出すこと。

入口周りと生活環境は，光，水，色彩の連続的な体験ができるように構成されている。リビング，ダイニング，プール，寝室にはそれぞれ異なった雰囲気が生まれ，風景，中庭，空が繋がっていく。

タイル葺きの屋根，木製梁，プラスター塗りの赤い壁，プール・タワーの石などが建物に個性を与えている。

家具，扉，把手，付属品から最後のディテールに至るまで，インテリア・デザインもすべて我々の手で行なった。ランドスケープも同様である。

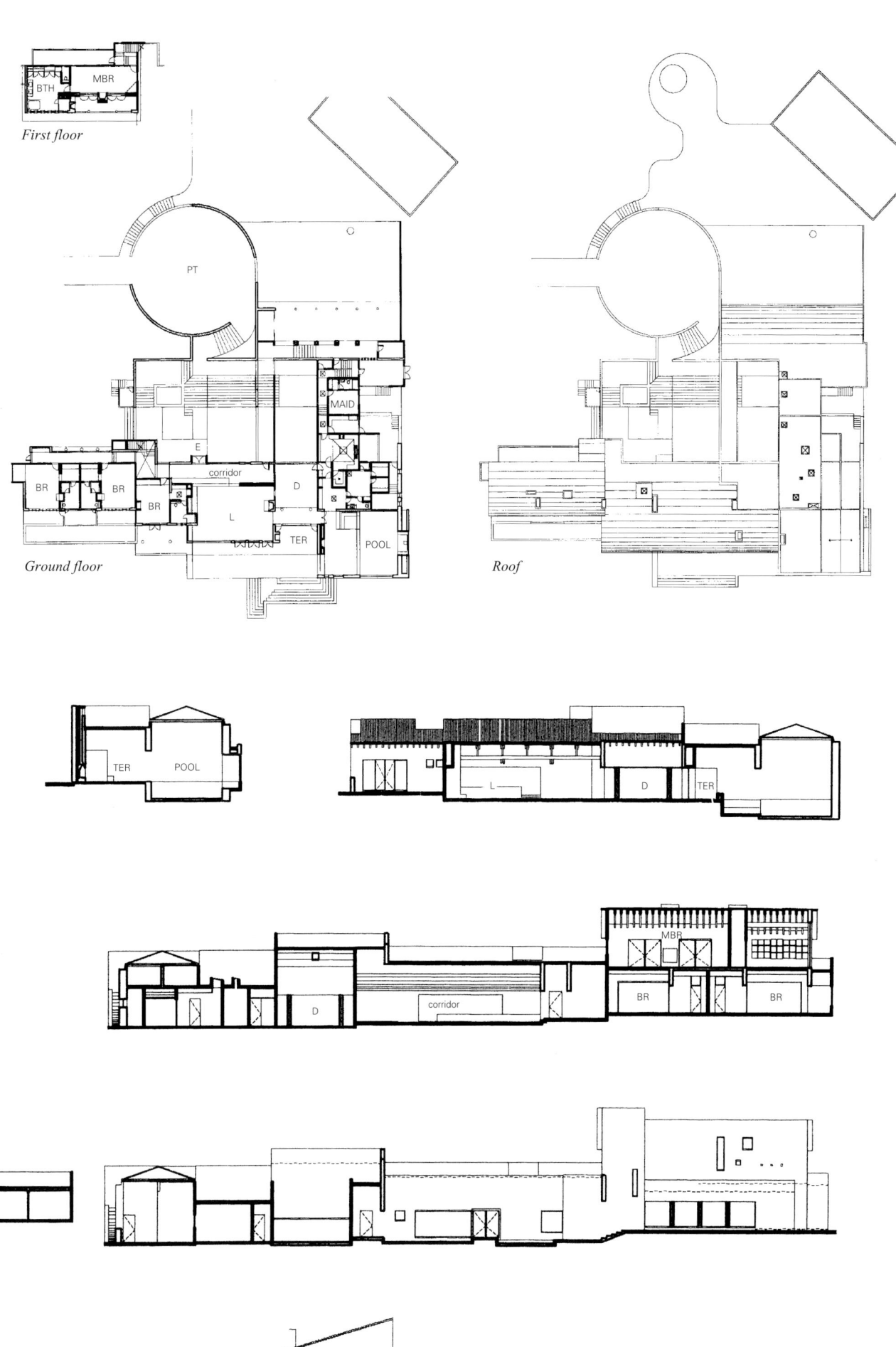

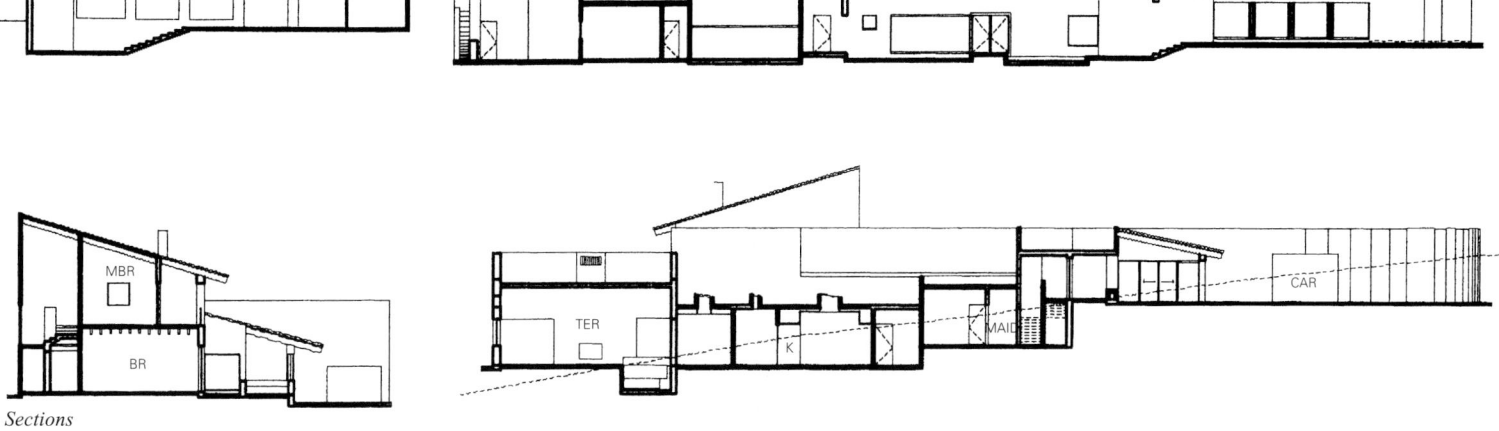

First floor

Ground floor

Roof

Sections

△▽*Living room* 居間

Corridor along living room　居間脇の廊下

Corridor to bedroom　寝室への廊下

Bedroom　寝室

Master bathroom　主浴室

Bedroom 寝室

Corridor: living room on left 廊下：左に居間

Bedroom 寝室

Master bedroom 主寝室

View toward pool over wall 壁越しにプールを見る

Pool プール

Ricardo Legorreta Ricardo Legorreta's House

Mexico City, Mexico, 1996–97

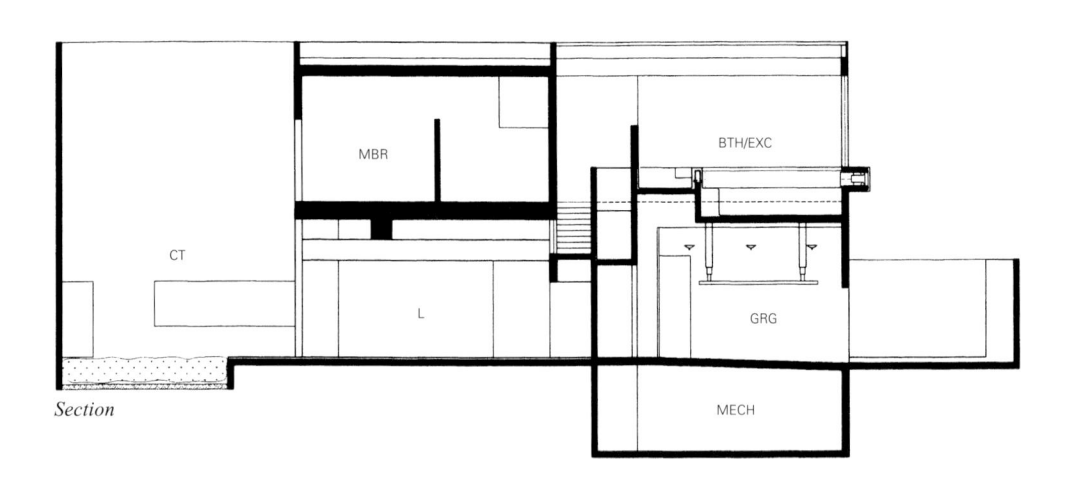

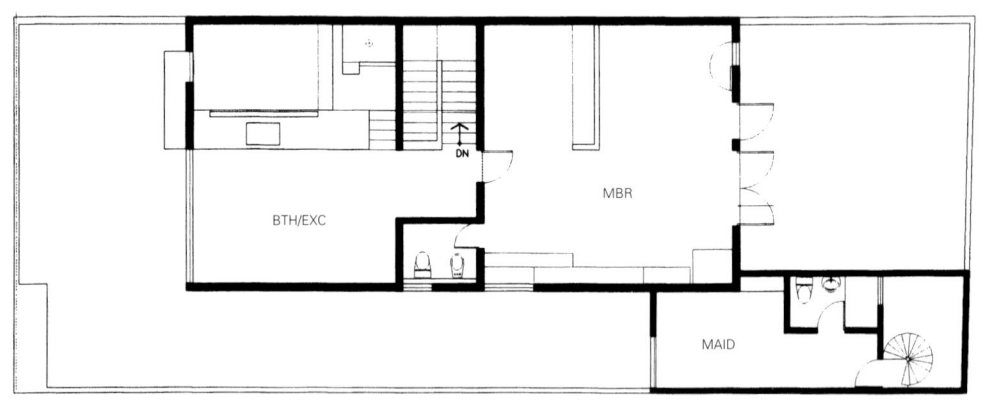

Section

First floor

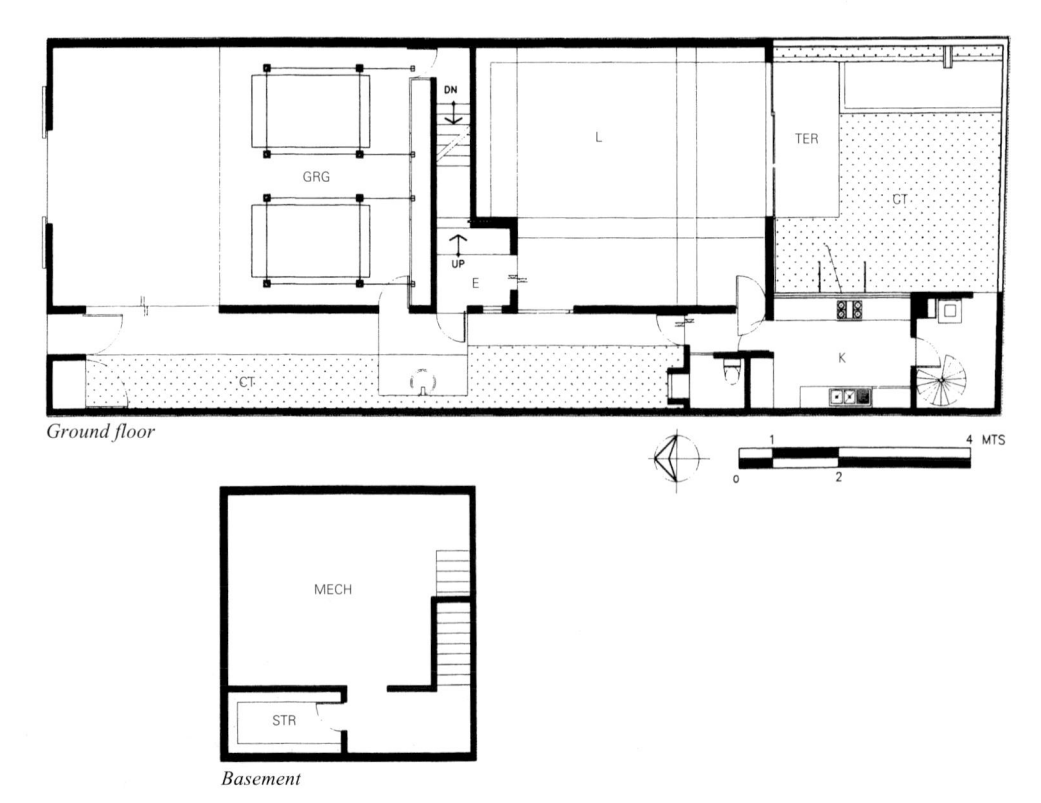

Ground floor

Basement

The house has been designed for the requirements of contemporary lifestyle of a single person in an urban environment. Most of the time the arrival is done by automobile so the garage is more of a vestibule than a conventional garage; through ingenious platforms it is possible to park four cars, two on top of the others.

The central space faces a courtyard with a fountain, a tree and red earth floor offering the right environment for conversation, reading, working and eating with flexibility and privacy.

A narrow stair gives access to the exercise room, resembling a courtyard with a sliding glass roof and views towards magnificent trees on the street. In this space exercise, swimming, showering and bath take place in an informal, simple and elegant way.

The four walls of the bedroom are covered with shelves and closets, filled with books and objects of daily use, the bed and reading sofa complete the furniture. Natural and artificial light offers a variety of effects through shutters, painted glass window and lamps.

Nothing in the house is decoration all the objects are part of the daily life. Space, color and light are used to create a romantic and spiritual retreat that protects from the chaotic urban life of the big city.

都市環境のなかで一人暮らしをする人の現代的生活スタイルの要求に基づいてデザインされた住宅である。住み手は，ほとんど車で帰宅するため，ガレージは通常のガレージというよりも玄関であると言った方がよい。創意工夫されたプラットフォームによって，2台の上に2台の車を重ね，計4台の車が収容できる。

中央の空間は，噴水や木があり，赤い土床の広がるコートヤードに面している。そこは，会話や読書，仕事をしたり，食事をしたりするのに適した，柔軟性に富み，プライバシーも守られる場所となる。

幅の狭い階段がエクササイズ・ルームへ繋がっている。この部屋にはスライド式のガラス屋根がかかり，通りの大木が見え，中庭のようである。ここでは，気軽に気取らず，かつ優雅に，体操や水泳をし，シャワーや風呂をつかうことができる。

寝室の4面の壁は，本や日用品でいっぱいになった棚やクローゼットで覆われている。ベッドと読書用のソファで家具は全てである。自然光や人工照明による光は，よろい戸や彩られたガラス窓，ランプによって多彩なものとなる。

この住宅に装飾的なものは何もない。全ての物が日常生活の一部である。大都市の混沌とした環境から保護された，空想的で精神的な避難場所をつくりだすために，空間，色彩，光が使われている。

Interior elevation

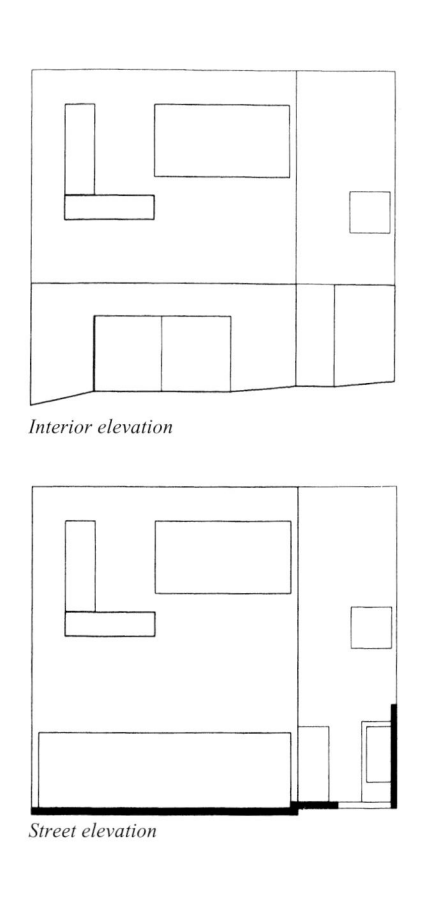

Street elevation

View from street 通りより見る

Courtyard: view toward living room 中庭：居間側を見る

Courtyard: view toward kitchen 中庭：台所側を見る

View toward entrance: garage on right　入口：右に車庫

Staircase　階段

Bedroom　寝室

Living room　居間△▽

View toward entrance　玄関を見る

129

Living room: looking courtyard　居間：中庭を見る

Exercise room　エクササイズ・ルーム

Bathroom 浴室

Bathroom 浴室△▽

Ricardo Legorreta Casa Cabernet

Napa Valley, California, U.S.A., 1996–98

It is intended to be a retreat house located on a 87 acres site in St. Helena, California, situated at 900 feet above the valley. The house faces south to take advantage of the views and the 30 acres of Cabernet Sauvignon planted five years ago.

The aim is to have a house that adapts to the surroundings, the existing trees and the climate. The house was divided in four different pavilions in order to integrate architecture with nature and trying to create a sense of intimacy and romanticism all spaces.

Family life is created in a unified space of the living, dining and kitchen areas. A different atmosphere and personality is created in each of the bedrooms due to the different types of windows, finishes and patios. Plastered and stone walls combine in order to enhance the overall design.

The result is an abstract compositions of walls and towers that will bend in a landscape with a series of oak trees.

South elevation

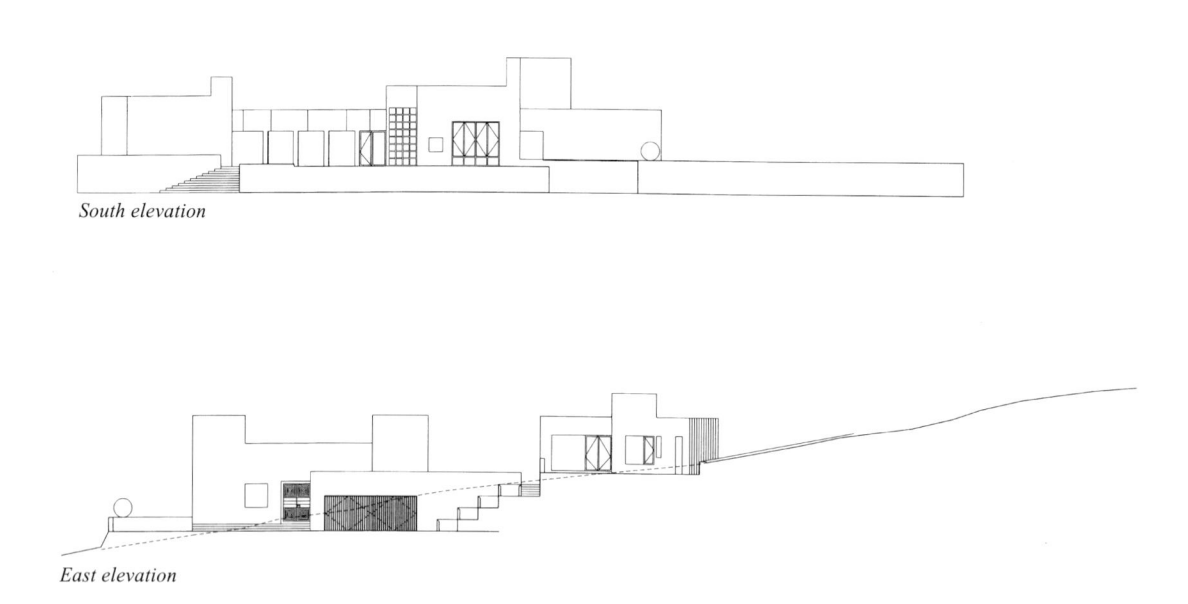

East elevation

カリフォルニア州セント・ヘレナにある87エーカーの敷地に建つ別荘で、谷底から900フィート上に位置する。家は眺望のよい南を向き、5年前に植えられたカベルネ・ソーヴィニヨン種の葡萄畑が前に広がっている。

周辺環境、既存の木立、土地の気候に合わせた家とすることを意図した。自然と融合させるために建物は4棟のパヴィリオンに分割され、各空間に親密にロマンチックな雰囲気が生まれるように工夫されている。

家庭生活の場はリビング、ダイニング、キッチンがまとめられた一室空間である。異なった雰囲気や個性は、窓、仕上げ、パティオの性格を変えることでそれぞれの寝室につくりだされている。全体的なデザインを強調するためにプラスター塗りと石の壁が組み合わされている。

結果は、カシの木立のある風景に添うように、壁とタワーが抽象的な構成を描くものとなった。

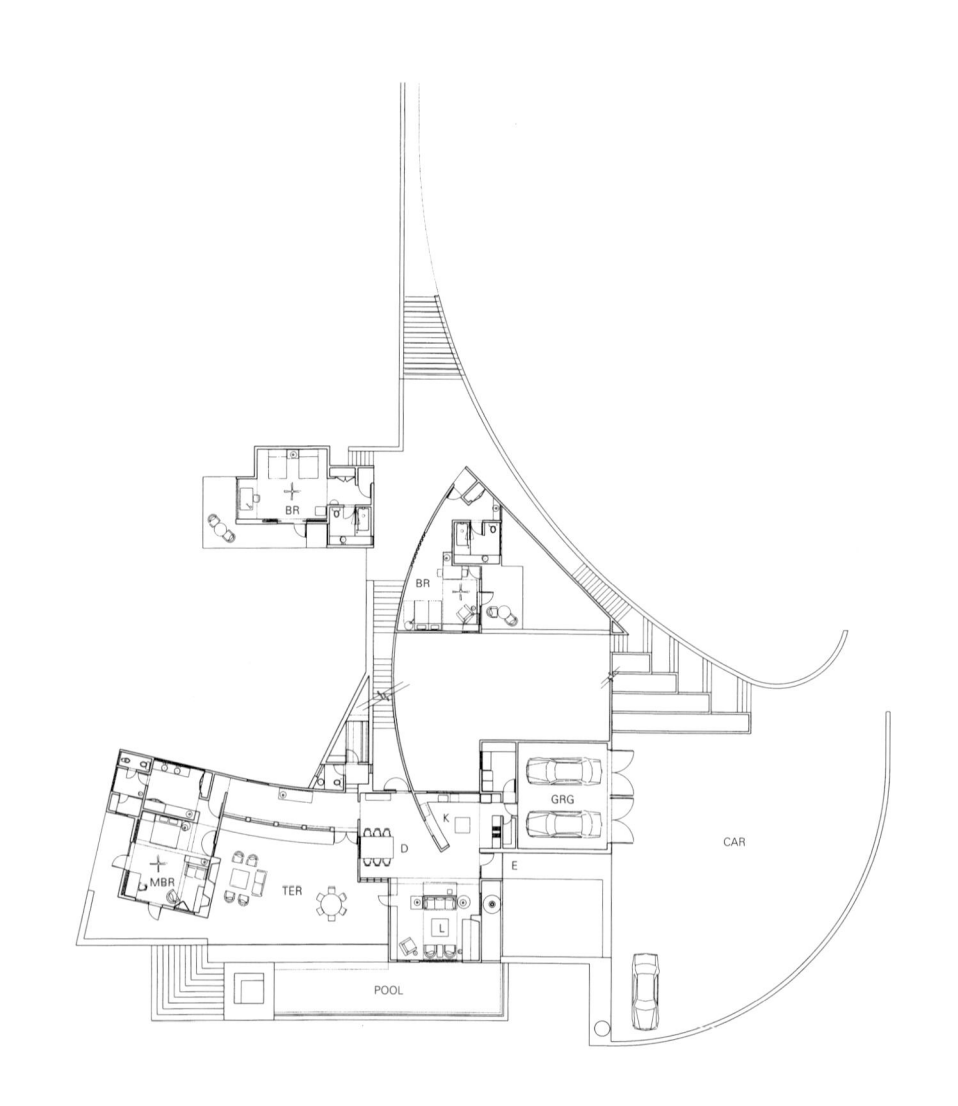

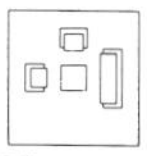

Plan

Sections

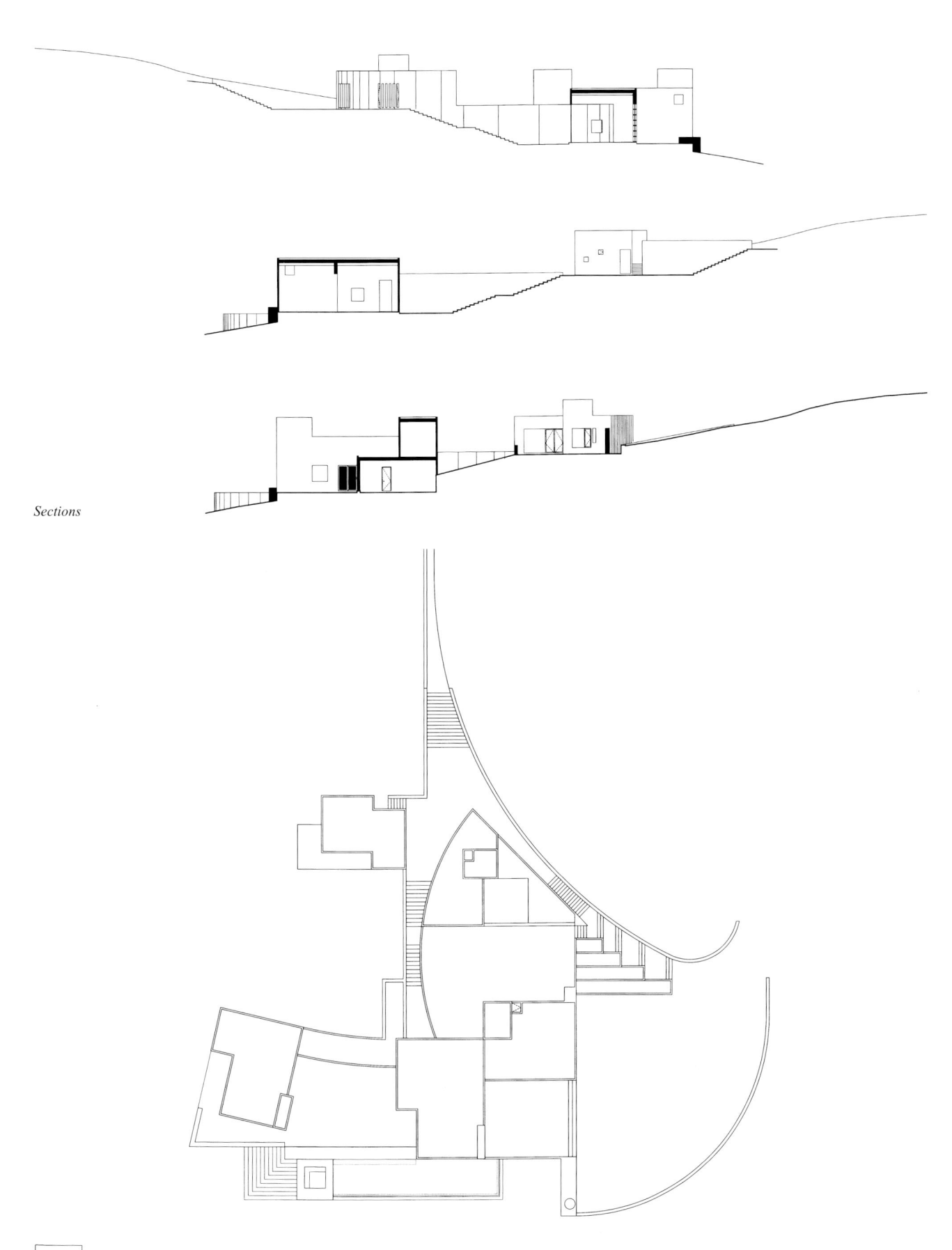

Roof

135

East elevation　東面

South elevation　南面

Entrance　玄関

Terrace on south　南側のテラス

137

Pool on south　南側のプール

Living/dining room　居間／食堂

View toward kitchen over wall　壁越しに台所を見る

Dining room　食堂

Portico　回廊

Living room: fireplace　居間：暖炉

△▽▷ *Bedrooms*　寝室

141

Enrique Norten House 'O'

Bosques de las Lomas, Mexico City, Mexico, 1990–91

The house is located along a busy boulevard in a newly developed elite suburb of Mexico City. A vacant lot on a larger piece of property, the site begins with an existing 12 meters high retaining wall. The lot measures approximately 21 meters wide and 8 meters deep with a 3 meters setback at the street facade and lateral ends. Eucalyptus forests to the north and east create natural edges on both sides of the street.

The program called for a single family house to accommodate a young couple. Exposure to the boulevard, however, provoked a closed expression of the street side facade in favor of a private, quiet, introspective place.

Composed of a series of planes, the house is to be experienced in the context of movement. Beginning with the existing retaining wall, these detached surfaces, each maintaining a unique material, color, shape and geometry define an overlapping of spaces that relate to the dynamics of the street. Lodged between two interior planes, the living and bedroom spaces occupy the second and third levels. Service facilities and circulation spaces are inserted along the outermost layers forming the main facade. In direct contact with the exterior, additional service spaces, a laundry room and parking occur at street level.

The dislocated planes subsequently orient the house parallel to the street, elongating perspectives to the outside. Patios, located at both ends of the house, provide natural ventilation and light creating a sense of spatial and visual continuity with the surrounding forests.

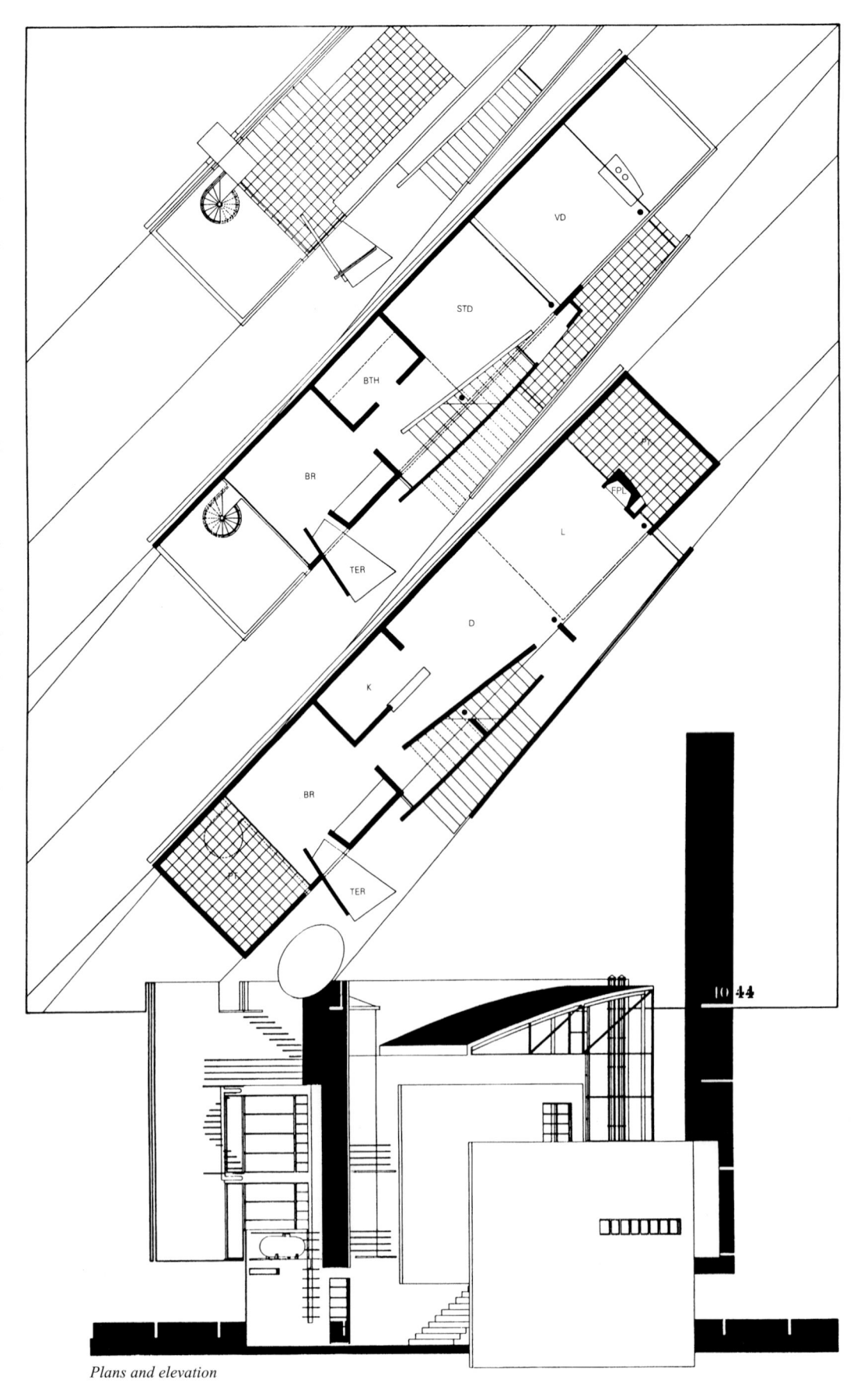

Plans and elevation

この住宅は，メキシコシティの新しく開発された高級住宅地域にある，交通量の多い大通り沿いに位置している。地所内の大きな区画にある空地を敷地とし，12メートルの高さが保たれた既存の壁から始まる。用地はおよそ21メートル幅と8メートルの奥行きがあり，通り側と隣地側に3メートルのセットバックがある。北側と東側に広がるユーカリの森は，通りの両側に自然な境界をつくりだす。

若いカップルにふさわしい一家族の住まいが要求された。大通りに面していることが，プライベートを保ち静かで内省的な場所になるように，通り側のファサードの閉じた表現を誘発した。

壁の連続からなるこの住宅は，動きのコンテクストの中において体験できる。既存の壁を始めとして，これらの分離した壁面は，ユニークな素材，色彩，形態と幾何学を固持しつつ，通りのダイナミズムと関係する空間の重なり合いを明らかにする。二つの内部の壁の間に置かれたリビングと寝室が2，3階を占める。サービスの機能とサーキュレーション・スペースはメインのファサードを形づくる一番外側の壁に沿って挿入される。外部に直に接する付加的なサービス・スペースや洗濯室，駐車場が通りのレベルを占める。

ずらされた壁は，外観のパースを引き延ばしながら，住宅の通りに対する平行性を方向づけている。住宅の両端に位置するパティオによって，周囲の森との空間的で視覚的な連続感を生みだす自然換気と採光が与えられている。

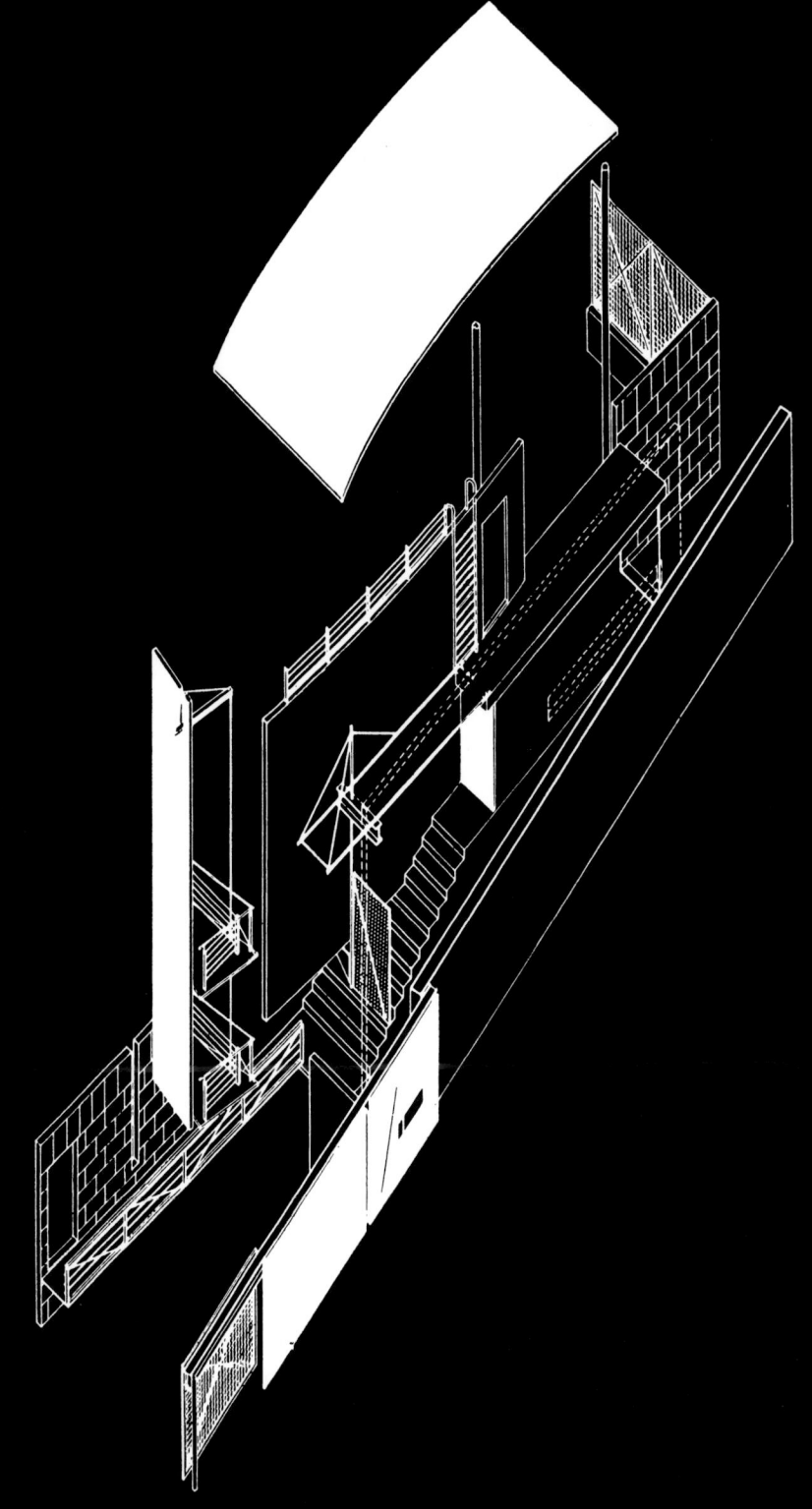

RM・15

Isometric

△▽*View from street* 通りより見る

View toward entrance　玄関を見る

Dining room 食堂

Studio スタジオ

Living room: looking patio through glazed wall　居間：窓越しにパティオを見る

Glazed canopy above entrance　玄関の上に掛かるガラス製キャノピー

Staircase　階段

TEN Arquitectos House R.R.

Mexico City, Mexico, 1996–97

A single family house located in a residential area of townhouses in the southern suburbs of Mexico City. The site is a 17 x 21 meter slot of space sharing party walls with its neighbors, and the short end of one of the continuous facades create the defined street wall typical of this townhouse neighborhood type.

The site is divided in two along its longitudinal axis as a consequence to its pronounced level variation and orientation. It has in the lowest part a three floor structure, which creates an intimate outdoor patio; providing southern exposure to the house as well as privacy from the street and neighboring houses. The disposition of the patio along with the rest of the house creates a "L" shape plan solution.

The program and budget called for a rational, straightforward organization. The spaces of the house are defined by the superimposition of parallel layers in both directions (north-south, west-east). Each layer expresses itself by its own materiality and tectonic solution, creating a virtual transparency.

Following the "L" shape plan: on the short side and in the middle level, are located the access and the principal living with a double height; perpendicular to it, dining, kitchen, breakfast room, service room and the lower part of the studio, facing the patio and the lap pool which runs along the lot in the same axis of the stairs which are contained in a transparent-glass volume. The portico is the transition between indoors and outdoors.

In the upper floor are located the family room, followed by a glazed bridge to the bedrooms and the upper part of the studio, as part as the master bedroom. The southern sun is blocked by a system of louvers in another plane parallel to the glass facade, providing privacy to the bedrooms. The ground floor contains the garage, service entry and laundry.

この一戸建ての住宅は，メキシコ市の南側の郊外に位置する，タウンハウスの並ぶ住宅地区にある。間口17メートル，奥行21メートルの細長い敷地は，両隣と境界壁を共有し，切れ目なく続く短手側の壁は，周辺のタウンハウスに典型的に見られる，壁を立てたような特徴のある街路側ファサードを構成している。

明快なレベル差があることや方位を考え，敷地を長手軸に沿って二分した。敷地の一番低い部分に3層の棟を置き，前面に小さな屋外パティオをつくる。パティオは家の南面を開放し，道路や隣家からのプライバシーを守ってくれる。パティオと3層棟に鍵の字につながる棟からL型プランが生まれる。

プログラムと予算は，合理的で簡単な構成を必要としていた。住空間は，両方向（北—南，西—東）に沿って平行に重なる層によって規定されている。各層はヴァーチャルな透明性をつくりながら，それぞれの物質性と構造によって自らを表現する。

L型プランに従って，道路側に面して下階にはアクセスと2層吹抜のメイン・リビングがあり，これに直角に食堂，台所，ブレークファスト・ルーム，サービス，2層吹抜のスタジオが並び，パティオとラッププールに面している。プールは，透明なガラスの箱の中に収まった階段と同軸線上を敷地に沿って延びる。ポルティコは屋内と屋外の転換域である。

上階には家族用の居間があり，そこからガラスのブリッジを経て寝室，主寝室，主寝室の一部であるスタジオ上部へつながる。南の日差しは，ガラス面に平行して設置されたルーバーによって遮られ，ルーバーはまた寝室のプライバシーを守る。地上階にはガレージ，サービス・エントリー，ランドリーが置かれている。

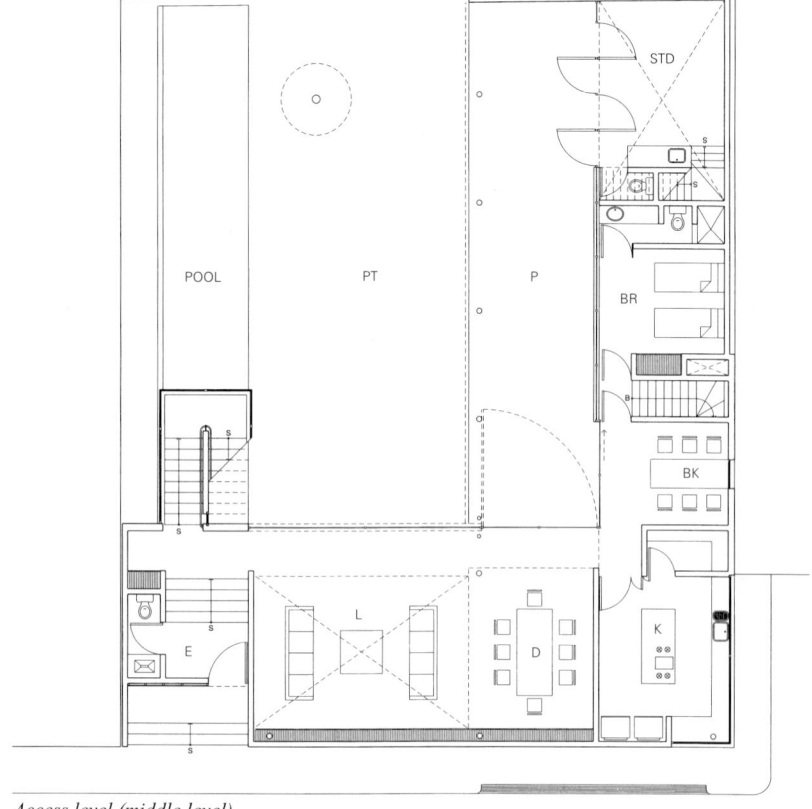

Access level (middle level)

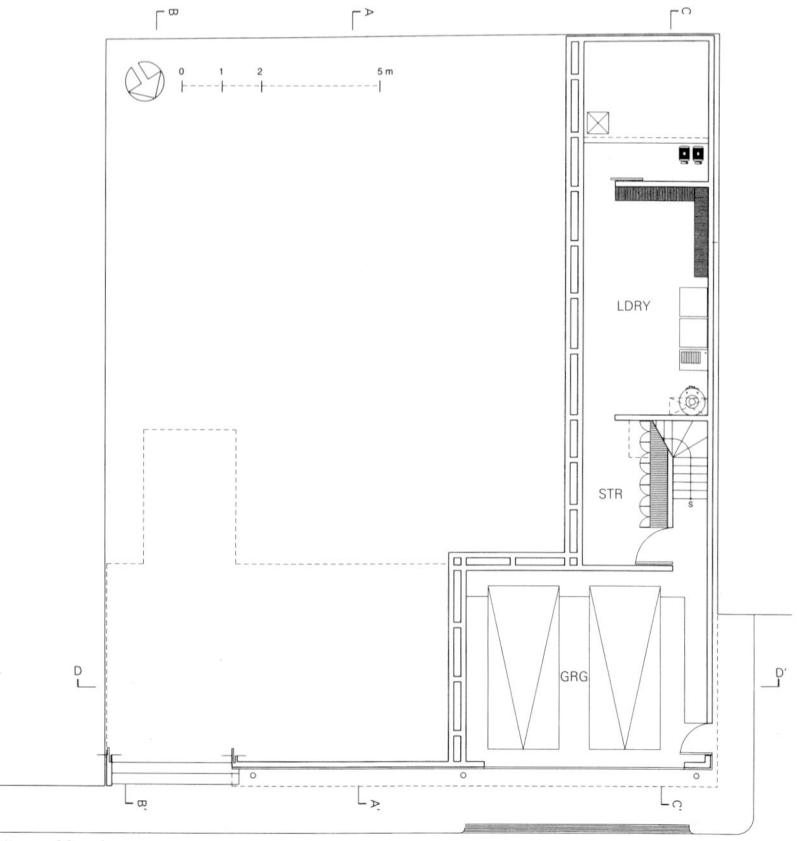

Ground level

Section A-A'

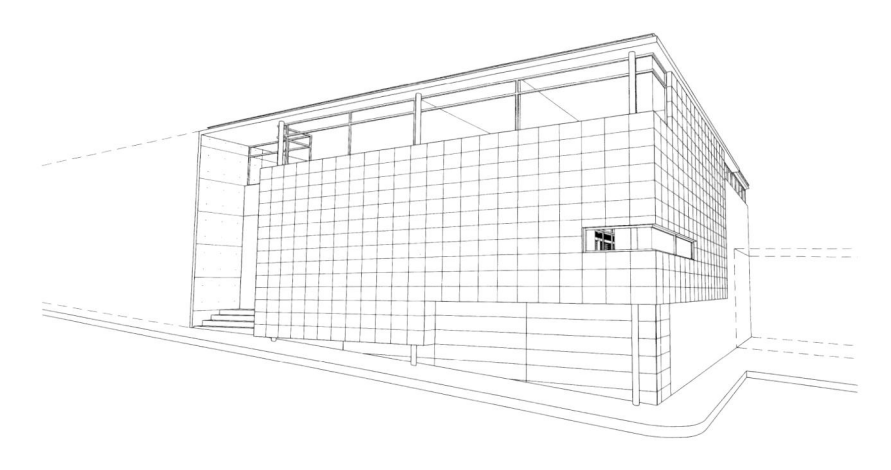

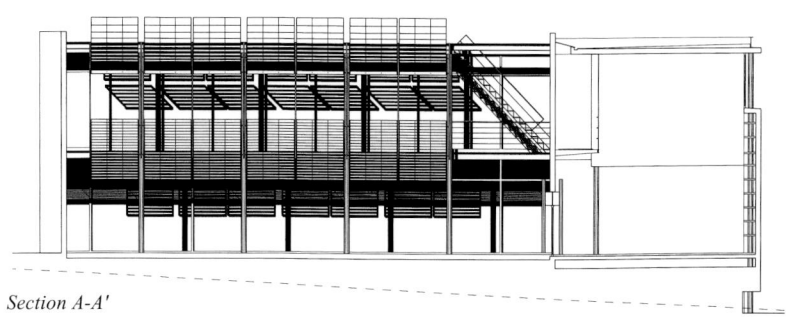

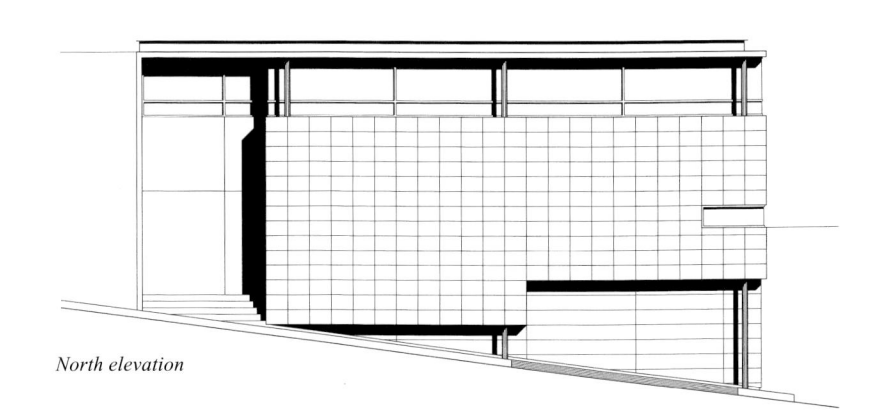

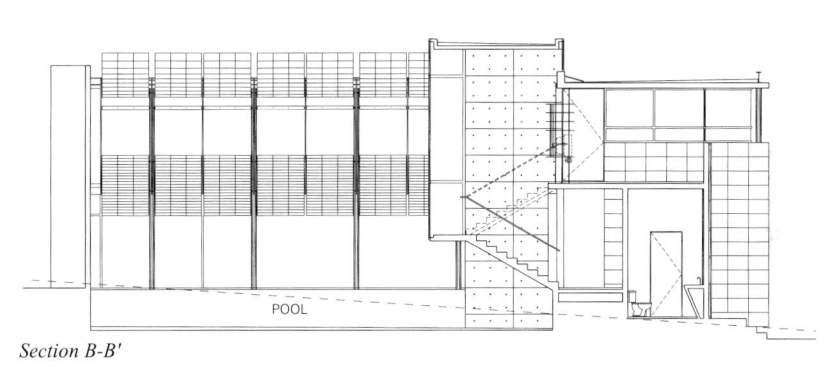

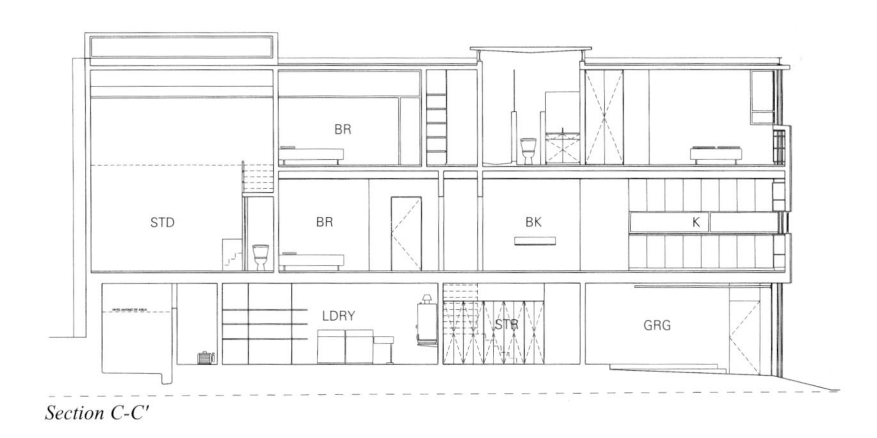

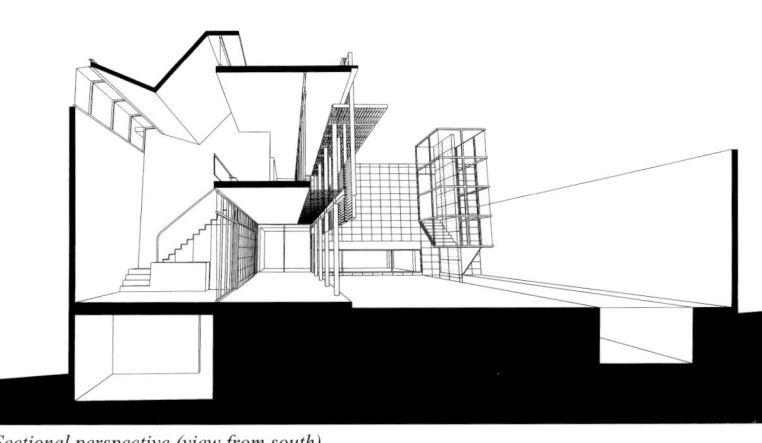

North elevation

Section B-B'

Section C-C'

Sectional perspective (view from south)

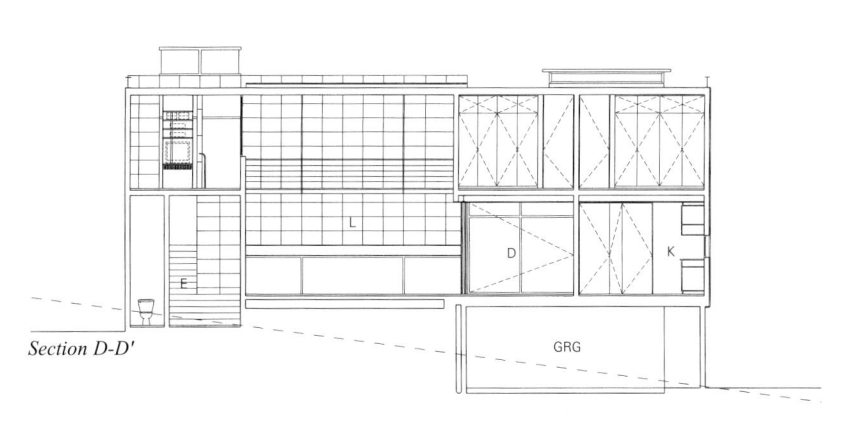

Section D-D'

151

East view　東面

View from north street　北側道路より見る

152

Glazed staircase　ガラス張りの階段室

Patio: view of north-south wing　パティオ：南北に延びる棟

Patio: view toward west-east wing. Portico on left　パティオ：東西に延びる棟を見る。左はポルティコ

Living room: corner detail　居間：隅部のディテール

Living room　居間

View toward portico from dining room　食堂よりポルティコを見る

Portico on upper level　上階のポルティコ

Master bedroom on upper level　上階の主寝室

Upper part of studio　スタジオの上階

Glazed bridge　ガラスのブリッジ

Alberto Kalach, Daniel Alvarez Negro House
Contadero, Mexico City, Mexico, 1994–97

Second platform on right and third platform on left　右に第2のプラットフォーム，左に第3のプラットフォーム

Entrance　玄関

Parking　駐車場

Terrace of third platform　第3のプラットフォームのテラス

Terrace of second platform　第2のプラットフォームのテラス

On a southern slope, on one of the many ravines of the west part of Mexico City, densely populated with tepozan trees, we visualized four structures in the form of large platforms floating in the landscape. Three of them are set upon pre-existing paths where the trees are less dense and the topography less precipitous.

Intended to disturb the environment as little as possible, the platforms follow the direction of the trails. Their foundations are condensed and imbedded in the earth, thus obviating sizable retaining walls and avoiding damage to the roots of the nearest trees. These foundations also comprise large cisterns; catching the rainwater channeled from roofs and patios, they seek self-sufficiency in water throughout the year.

The structures, then, are congenial to topography, vegetation and orientation, conciliating the simple and direct organization of all the spaces. Each structure retains its own rhythms and proportions in harmony to its functions, while reaffirming the unity emerging from the total topographical/structural conception.

The concrete, steel, wood and glass are married to achieve an organic unity of space, form and structure. The non structural walls made of sandy stone which is made of the same soil of the place (tepetate), give the texture and warmth to the house.

The first platform makes the entrance to the house through a small patio, followed by the living and dining room that opens to the view. From there, you can exit to the roof of the next platform which is a terrace and a water mirror that reflects both nature and architecture. Stepping down is the next element that contents the bedrooms and family room. From there you get out of the house to an open terrace or to the studio, that has two levels and also has the facilities for the swimming pool. Finally the swimming pool is a 25-meter-long lap, that as the rest of the house, is completely buried in the forest.

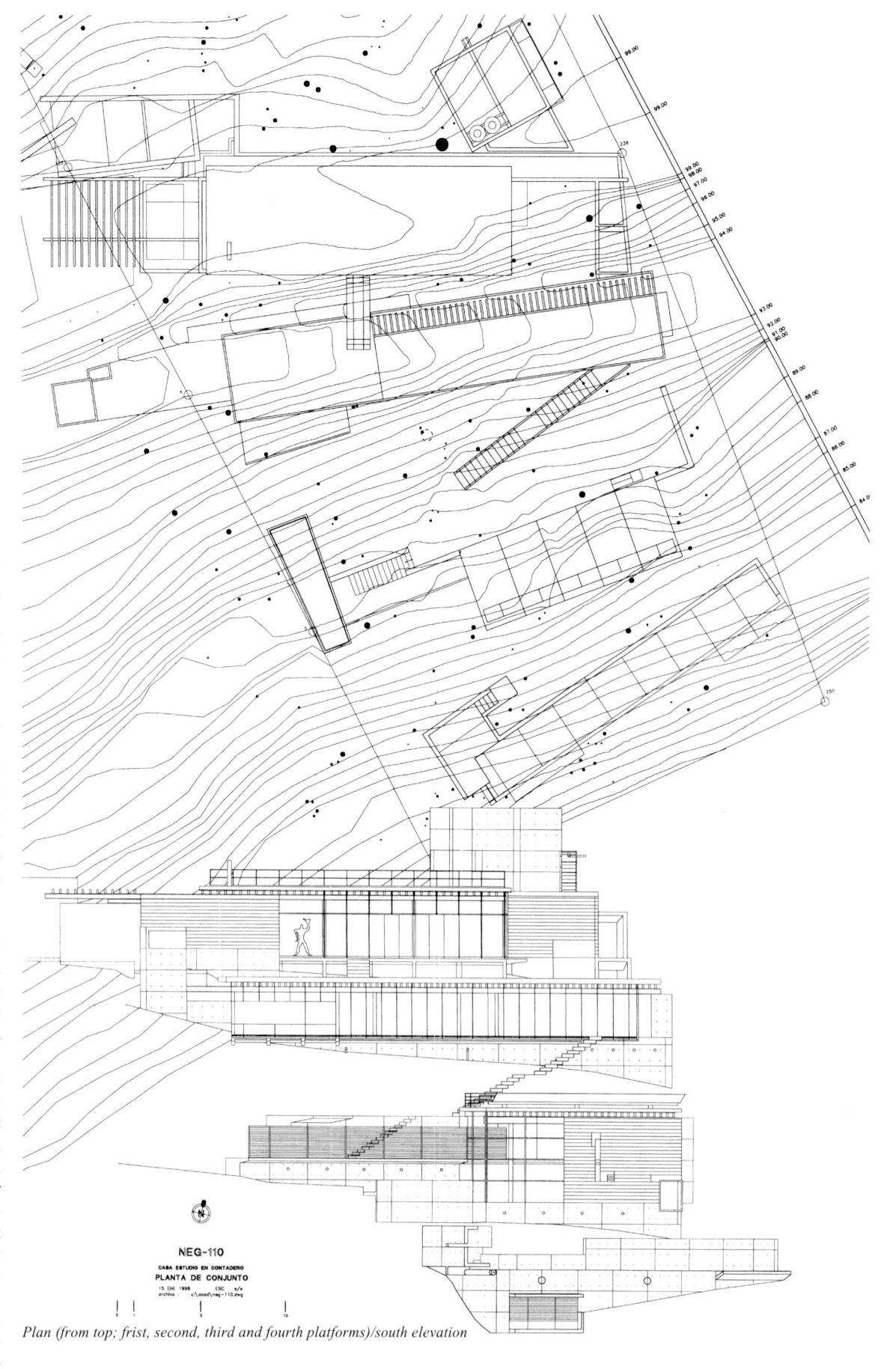

Plan (from top; frist, second, third and fourth platforms)/south elevation

メキシコシティ西部に数多く散在する峡谷の一つ。テポサンの木が生い茂るその南斜面に，風景の中に浮かぶように，プラットフォームの形をした大きな4つの建物が現れる。そのうち3つは，あまり地形が険しくなく，木もそれほど多くはない既存の小道に面して建てられている。

4つのプラットフォームは，できるだけ周辺の自然環境を乱さないように，小道の方向に沿って配置されている。建物の基礎は規模を縮小して地中に埋めることによって，大きな擁壁を不要とさせ，近くの木の根を傷めずにすむ。基礎には大きな水槽も併設され，屋根やパティオから雨水を導管で集めて，年間を通しての水の自給自足を目指している。

こうして，それぞれのプラットフォームは，地形，植生，方位に適合しつつ，すべての空間の簡潔で直接的な構成との調和をつくりあげる。それぞれは機能に応じて固有のリズムとプロポーションを持つ一方で，全体の地形的／構造的なコンセプトから生まれる統一性を主張してもいる。

コンクリート，スティール，木，ガラスは，空間や形態，構造と合わさって有機的な一体感をつくりだすように，緊密に結びつけられる。地元産の石でできた非構造壁は，住宅にテクスチャーと暖かみを与える。

第一のプラットフォームは，小さなパティオを経由するエントランスを構成し，見晴らしの良いリビングや食堂がそれに続く。そこから次のプラットフォームの屋上に出られる。そこには自然の景色や建築を映す鏡のような水面とテラスが広がっている。さらに階段を降りていくと，寝室と家族室があり，そこから住宅の外に出て斜面を下ると，オープン・テラスつまりスタジオに至る。この棟は2層で，スイミング・プール施設が付いている。プールは長さ25メートル，建物の残る部分は完全に森に姿を埋めている。

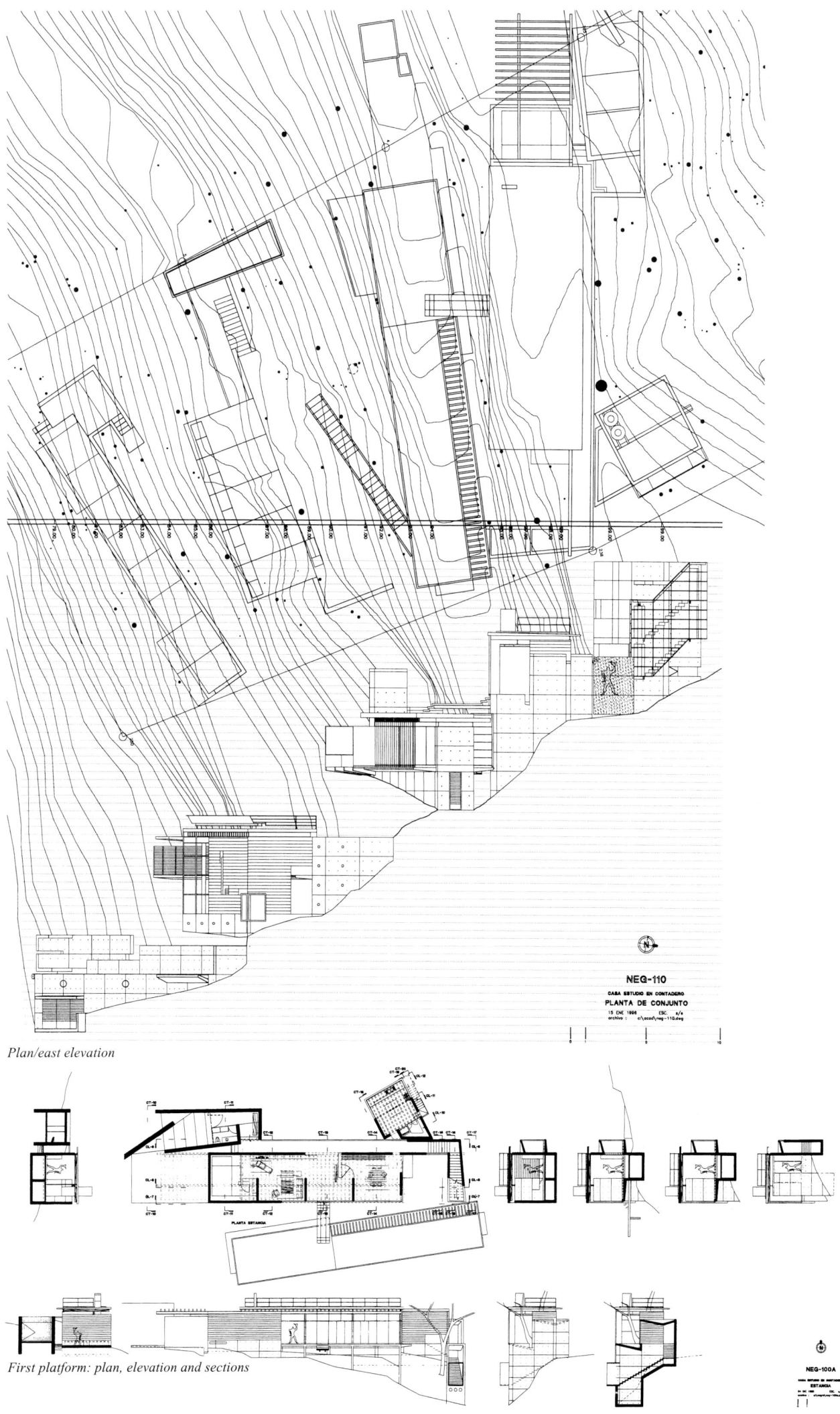

Plan/east elevation

First platform: plan, elevation and sections

Second platform (bedroom & family room)　第2のプラットフォーム（寝室と家族室）　　*View from first platform to second platform*　第1から第2のプラットフォームを見る

Living room　居間 　　*Dining room*　食堂

View of staircase from family room on second platform　第2のプラットフォームの家族室から階段を見る

Corridor on second platform
第2のプラットフォームの廊下

Master bedroom on second platform　第2のプラットフォームの主寝室

Studio on third platform 　第3のプラットフォーム，スタジオ

Third platform　第3のプラットフォーム

△▽*Studio* スタジオ

Downward view of terrace and pool on third and fourth platforms　第3，第4のプラットフォームのテラスとプールを見下ろす

Kitchen on first platform　第1のプラットフォームにある台所

Master bedroom on second platform　第2のプラットフォームの主寝室

Studio　スタジオ

Inbetween space of first and second platforms　第1と第2, 2つのプラットフォームの間

Downward view from third platform　第3のプラットフォームからの見下ろし

Swimming pool on fourth platform　第4のプラットフォームのプール

Alberto Kalach GGG House

Mexico City, Mexico, 1997–99

The house could be seen as the most simple and yet the most complex and exiting architectural theme. I understand it as a passage that transport their inhabitants from the every day life, the street, to an inner world of intimacy. The succession of spaces that are discovered always indirectly, diagonally or at a turn without being seen until you enter to each of them, are the scenario to compel the human act, but also they conform a plot in itself.

Its spatial idea, inspired in the work of the sculptor Jorge Yazpik, starts with a basic accommodation of the program, that allow afterwards, with more freedom, the exploration of spatial relations through clay models. Each indentation or cut in the mass suggest the next one, in a progressive work where the space is discovered rather than invented, until reaching the final volume.

The house is imagined as a great concrete monolith that is fragmented geometrically and progressively within a spatial network defined by the successive inscription of sphere within cube, and this within a sphere.

The light filters through the cracks as rays, but at times light explodes softly flooding the spaces. The shadows, the brightness and the penumbra, enliven the passages through the house and contrasts the spaces marking the time flow. Gardens, pools, patios, pavilions and alcoves, are linked by the cracks that break the monolith.

The general volumes of the house respond to the compelling location of the site, wedged between a beautiful golf course, a warehouse and a five story apartment building.

この住宅は，極めて単純でありながら，極めて複雑で刺激的な建築テーマを表現していると言えるだろう。私はこの家を，住む人を日常性や街路から，心地よい内部世界へ運ぶ通路であると理解している。連続していく内部空間は——その一つ一つに入るまで空間は知覚されず，常に間接的に，対角方向に，屈折点に発見される——人の動きを強要するためのシナリオであるが，また空間自身のもつプロットに従ってもいる。

こうした空間に対する考え方は，彫刻家ホルヘ・ヤスピクの作品に啓発されたもので，まずプログラムに対応する基本的な枠組みをつくってから，粘土模型によって，空間関係をさらに自由に探求して行くことができる。マッスに刻みや切り込みを入れて行くたびに次の切り込みへ導かれる。それは，最終的なヴォリューム構成に至るまで，空間を創造するというよりむしろ発見していく作業である。

この家は，幾何学形態によって次々に断片化されてゆく巨大なコンクリート・モノリスとして構想されている。そこでは，キューブのなかに球，キューブは球のなかにと，継続的に刻みこむことで構成された空間のネットワークが生まれている。

光は細い亀裂から光線の束となって浸透するが，ときどき，柔らかに広がって空間をあふれるように満たす。明と暗，そしてその境界域が家全体にわたって通路を生き生きさせ，時の流れを刻印しながら空間を対比させる。庭園，プール，パティオ，東屋，アルコーブはモノリスを破る亀裂によってつながれている。

この家の全体的なヴォリュームは，美しいゴルフコース，納屋そして5階建てのアパートの間に楔のように割り込んだ，制約の多い敷地のロケーションに対する解答である。

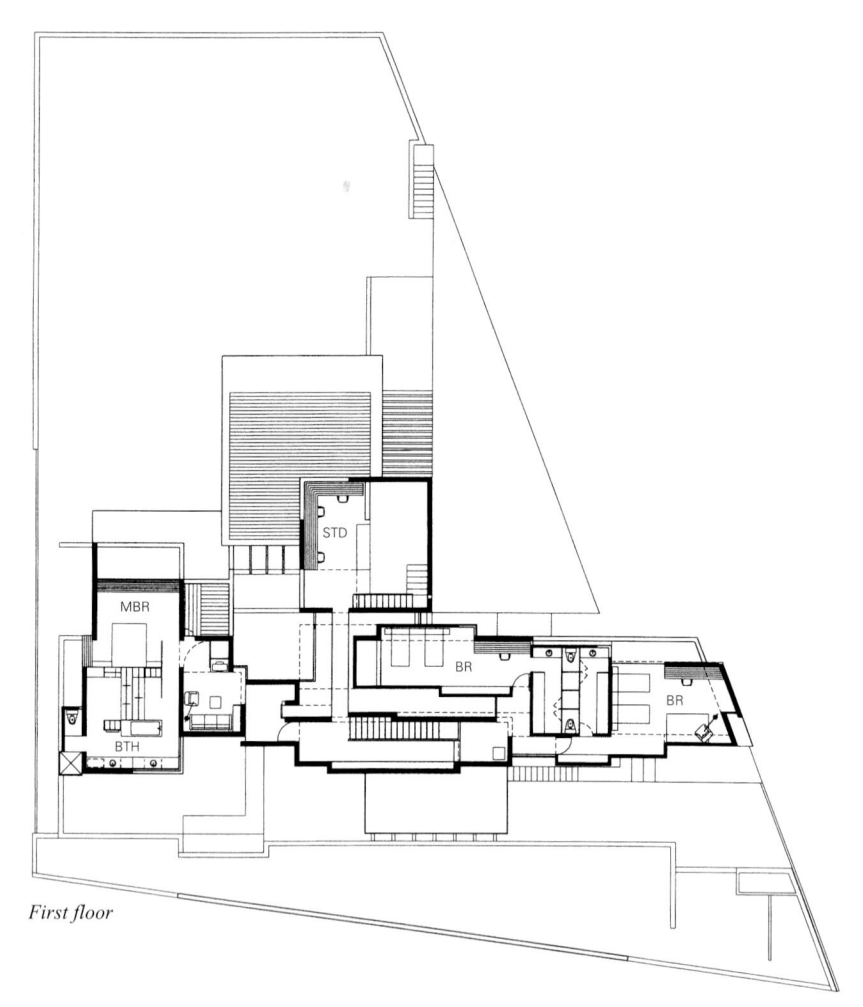

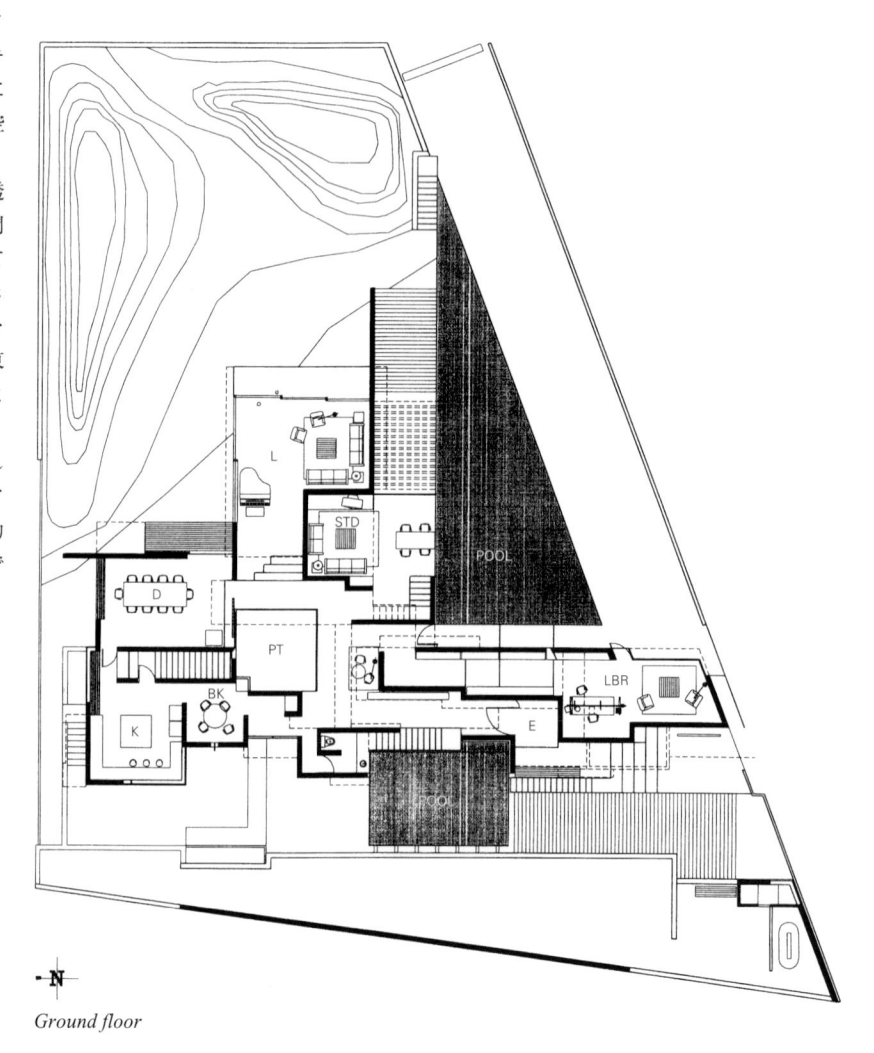

First floor

Ground floor

View from street on south　南側の道路より見る

East elevation: view toward living room　東面：居間を見る

Garden on west　西側の庭

View from south: entrance on right　南より見る：右に玄関

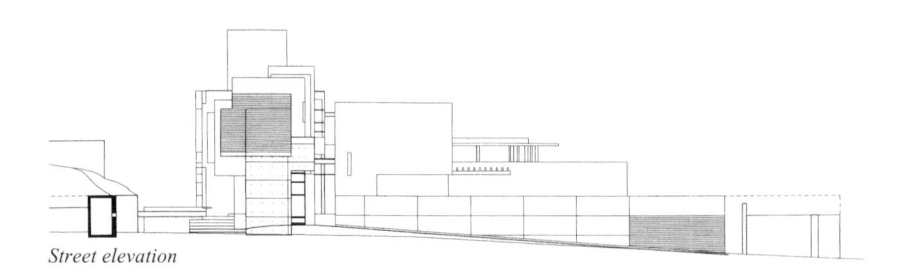

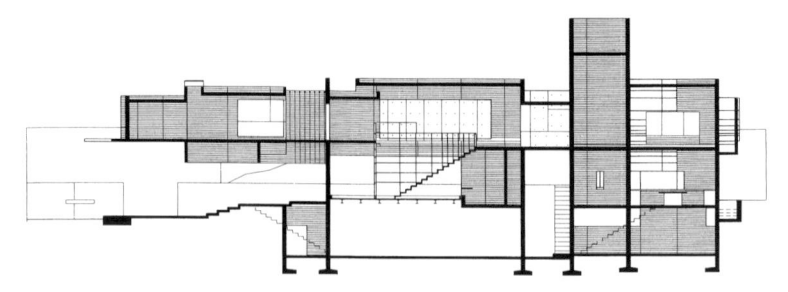

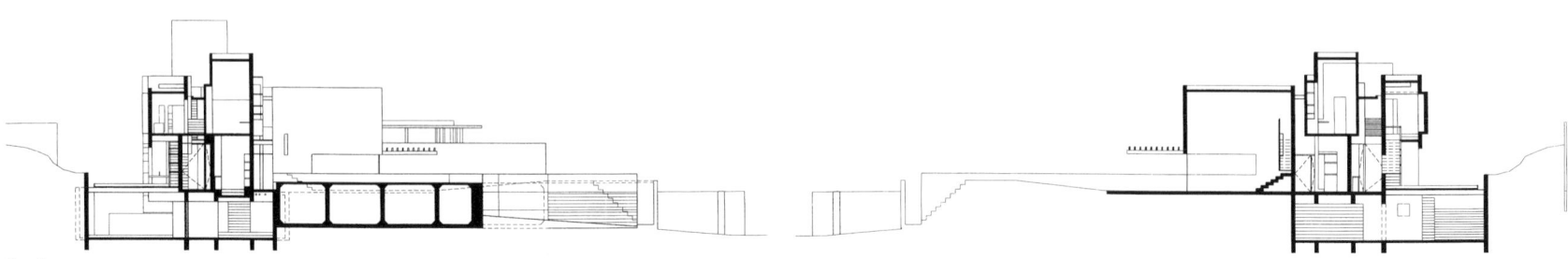

Street elevation

Sections

Hall: view from entrance　ホール：玄関より見る

Patio: living room on right　パティオ：右手奥は居間

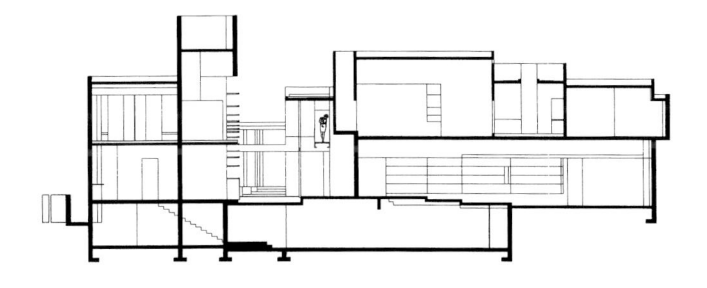

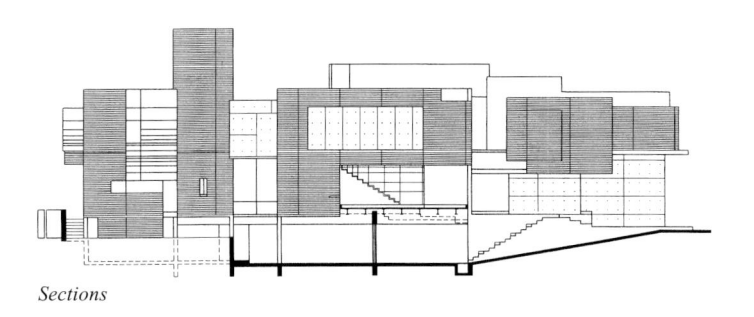

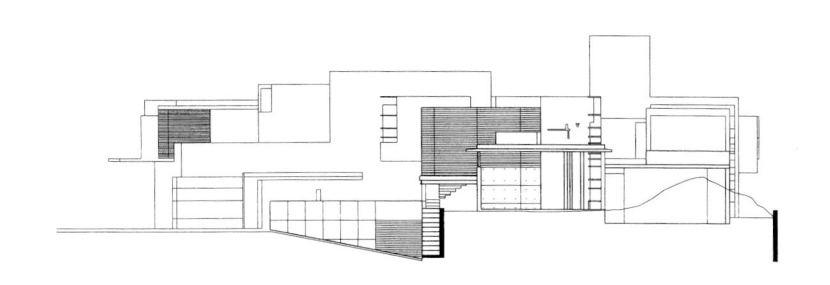

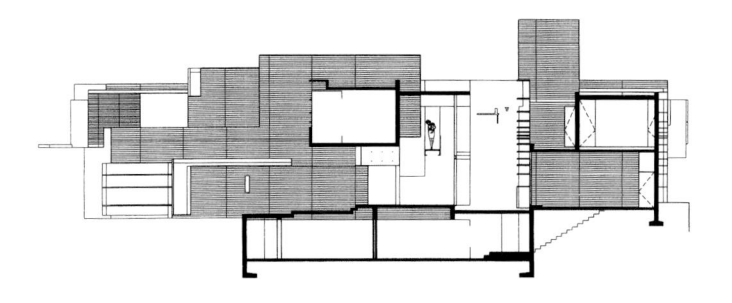

Sections

Patio　パティオ

△▷*Living room*　居間

172

Stair hall on first floor　2階，階段ホール

Window of bedroom: view toward pool　寝室の窓：プールが見える

Studio　スタジオ

Dining room　食堂

Glazed bridge: view toward studio ガラスのブリッジ：スタジオを見る

Glazed bridge ガラスのブリッジ

First floor: view toward hall from bedroom 2階：寝室よりホールを見る

View toward living room through patio from breakfast room
朝食室からパティオ越しに居間を見る

Roof terrace　屋上テラス

Master bedroom　主寝室

Grupo LBC Casa en Valle de Bravo
Valle de Bravo, Mexico, 2001–04

View from lakeside on north　北側の湖の方から見る

View from east: looking living room, terrace on right　東より見る：居間側を見る，右にテラス

Living room 居間△▽

The idea for the design of this house answers, above all, to the orientation and views that the site offers. Located in Valle de Bravo, in the state of Mexico, in a site with a dense vegetation and views over the lake of Valle de Bravo, the house is isolated from the main street by a change in levels in the access that allows for a more intimate environment in close relationship with the landscape. The use of local materials and the effort made to maintain the existing vegetation as well as the natural characteristics of the site bring about an exercise in conciliation between architecture and nature, between the ideas of contemporary and traditional construction in Mexico.

Three walls contain the terrain. Two independent pavilions, one joint to and the other supported on these walls, form and give sense to both architecture and terrain. The use of local stone and formal elements such as the roof, search for a contextual relationship with local constructions. The layout of the house allows for the conservation, in its original state, of an important part of the terrain.

The house is developed in a longitudinal sense defining the service and connecting spaces, the living spaces and the spaces from where the landscape can be enjoyed. In a tour of spaces that oscillates from intimacy to open views, one enters the house through a small plaza that results from the difference in levels between the access and the main street. Lit and heated by a skylight a distribution space also contains the service spaces. The bedrooms search, through a more intimate character, to be spaces of withdrawal and reflection but not forgetting its relationship with the exterior. In contrast, the public areas (dining room and living room) open up in a decisive and transparent way to the surprising views, extending themselves by ways of a cantilever structure that embraces the terrain, the landscape and the lake without altering them.

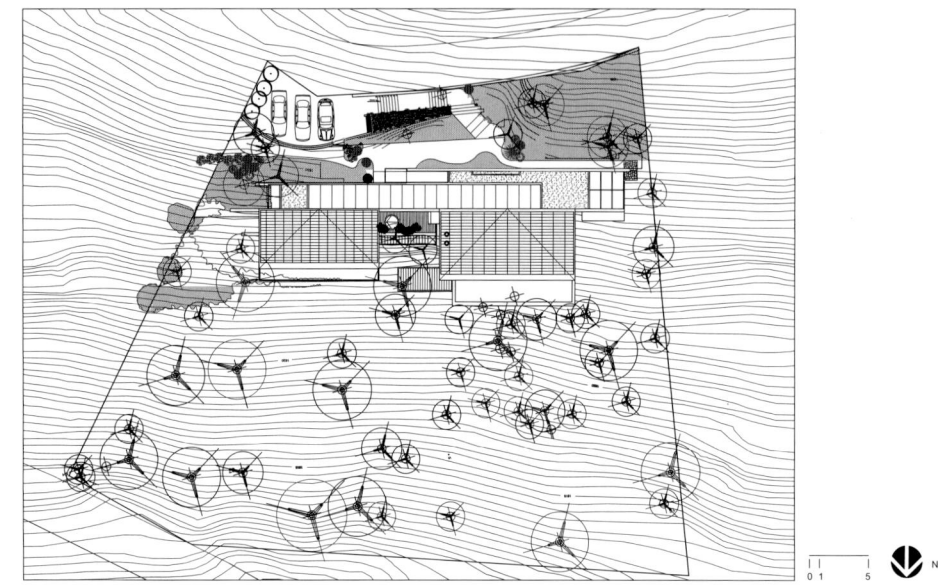

Site plan

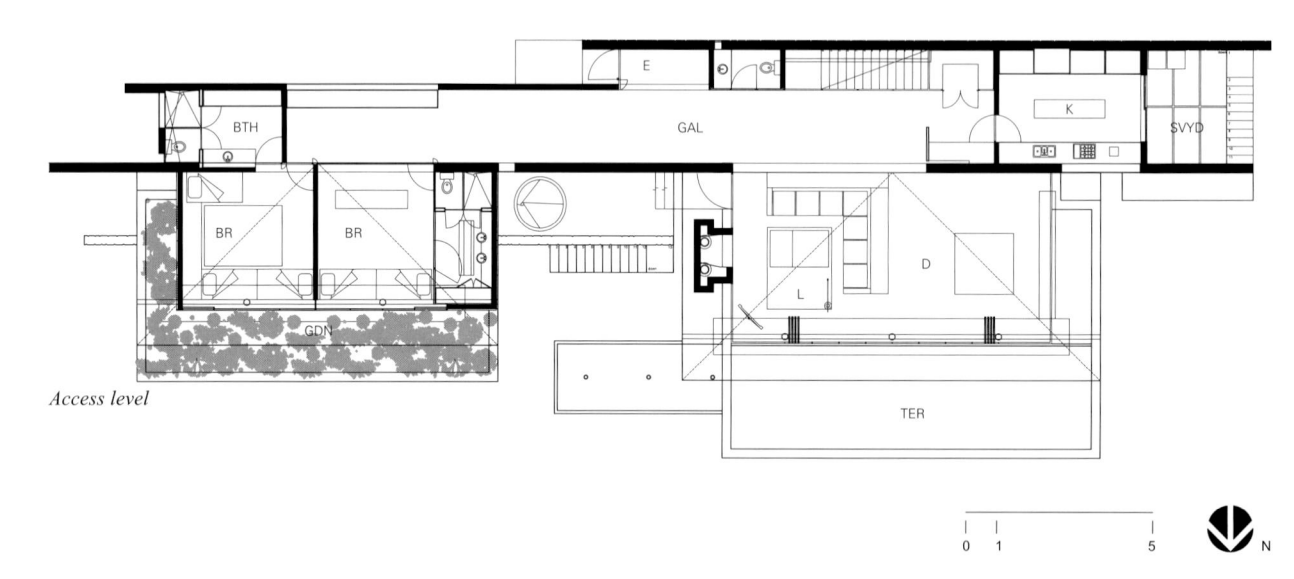

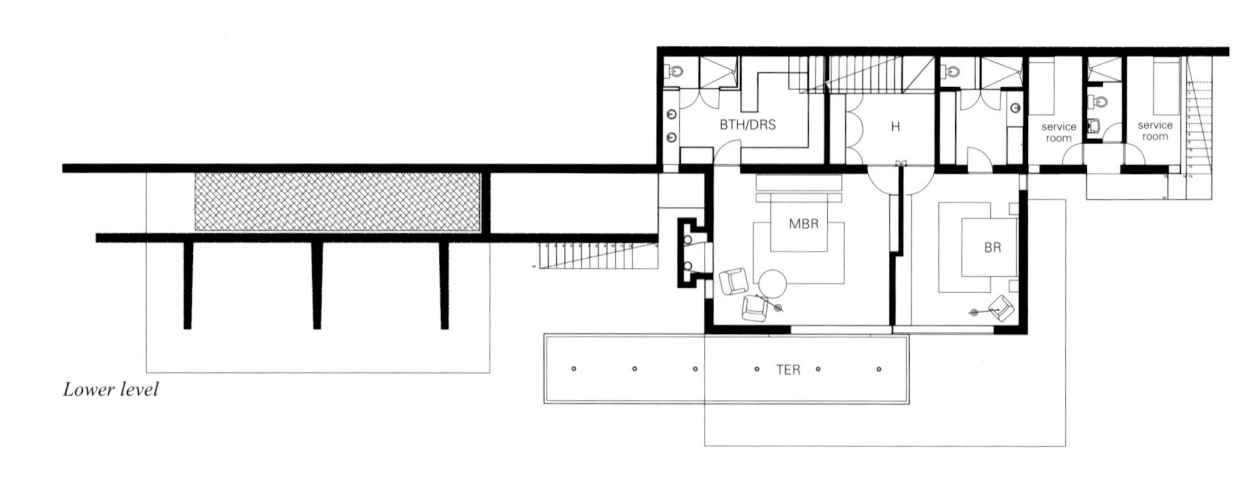

Access level

Lower level

South elevation

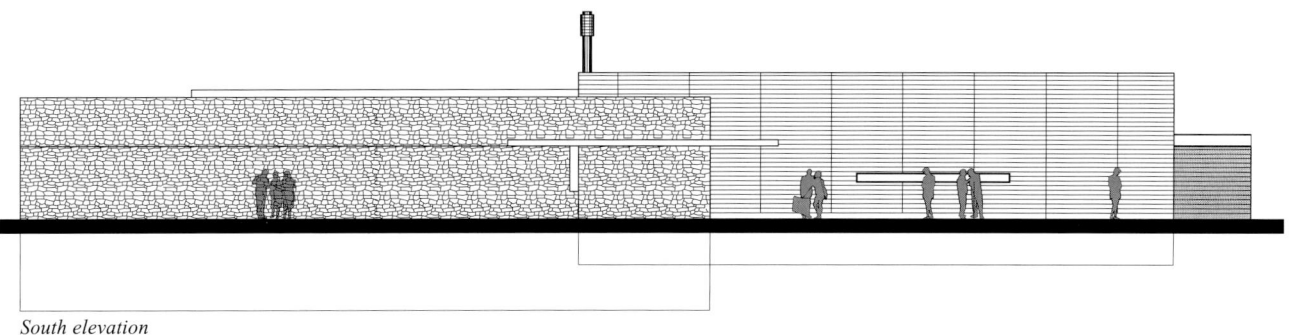

　この住宅のデザインは，何よりもこの敷地が与えてくれる方位と眺望に答えようとしたものである。メヒコ州のバイエ・デ・ブラボにある，草木が生い茂り，バイエ・デ・ブラボ湖が見晴らせる敷地で，進入路が上の道路から低く下に降りて行き，風景が身近に感じられる人目につかない環境に家が配置されている。地元の材料を使い，地域的な植生と敷地の自然を守る努力から，建築と自然，現代とメキシコの伝統建築を和解させようというデザインが生まれた

　3枚の壁が周囲一帯の地形を包み込む。一方はこれらの壁に連結し，他方はその上に支持された2つの独立したパビリオンが建築と土地の両方をかたちづくり，意味を与える。屋根などに地元の石材や形態要素を使用し，この地方の建物との文脈的な関係をつけている。家の配置にあたっては，地形上の重要な部分を，当初のままに保つことに注意した。

　内部空間はサービスと各部屋を結ぶ通路，リビング・スペース，そして風景を楽しめるスペースなどが長手方向に配置されている。間近な眺めから開放的な眺めの間を揺れ動く空間の旅のなか，進入路と上の道路の高度差から生まれた小さな広場を抜けて家のなかに入る。通路スペースにはスカイライトから太陽の光と熱が降り注ぎ，サービス・スペースもここにある。寝室はこじんまりとした，引きこもって，沈思する空間になっているが，外部との関係も忘れられていない。対照的に，パブリック・エリア（食堂と居間）はキャンティレバーで外に張り出し，この土地，風景と湖の姿をそのままに抱きかかえ，直截明快な方法で素晴らしい眺めに対して開いている。

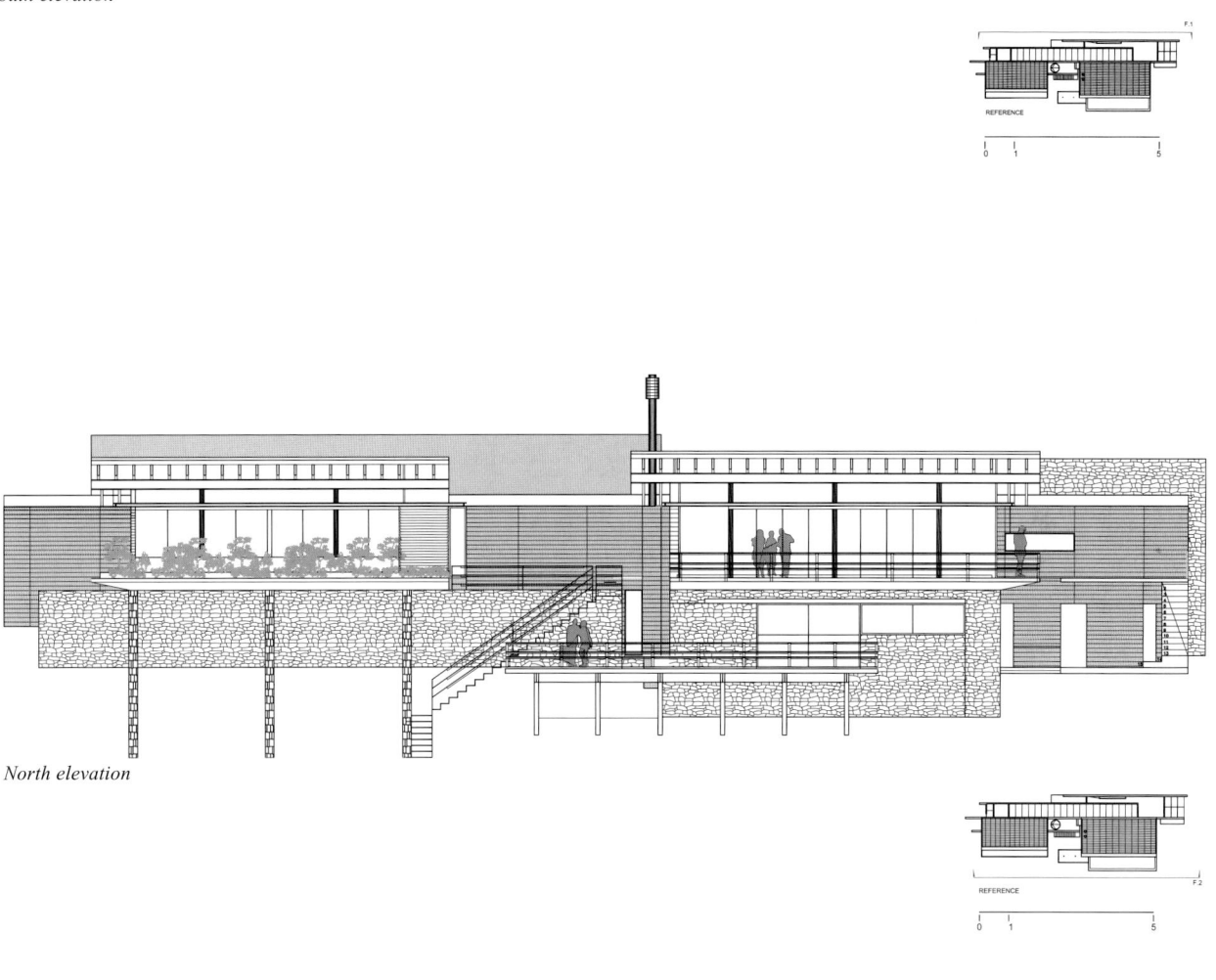

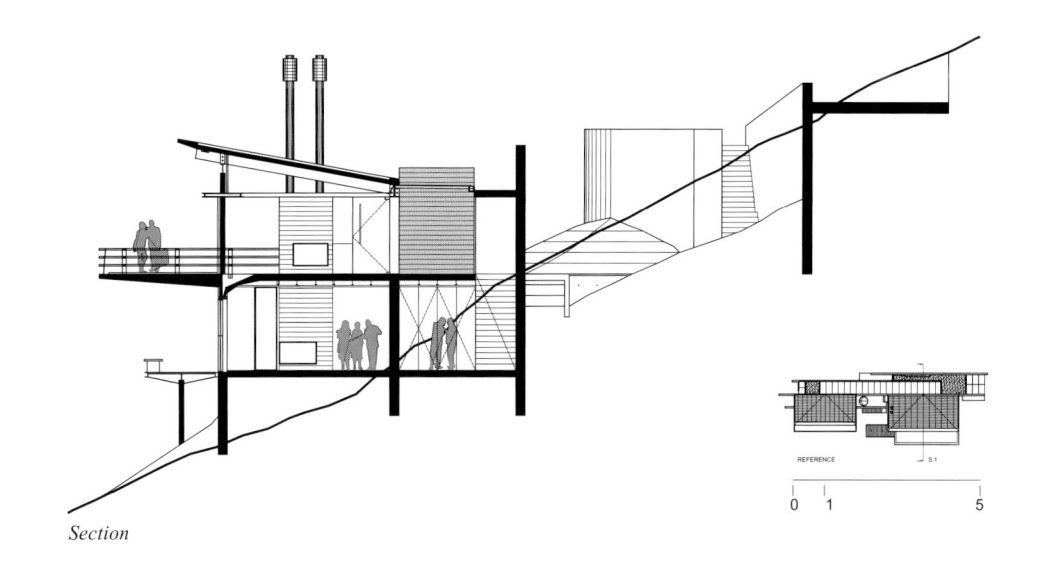

North elevation

Section

△▽*Gallery with skylight*　トップライトのあるギャラリー

Living room on left, kitchen on right　左に居間，右に台所

Northwest corner of kitchen/service yard　台所の北西角部

Northeast corner of bedroom on access level　アクセス階，寝室の北東隅部

BGP Arquitectura House GDL1

Guadalajara, Zapopan, Jalisco, Mexico, 2003–05

Overall view from south　南側全景

View from east　東より見る

South elevation

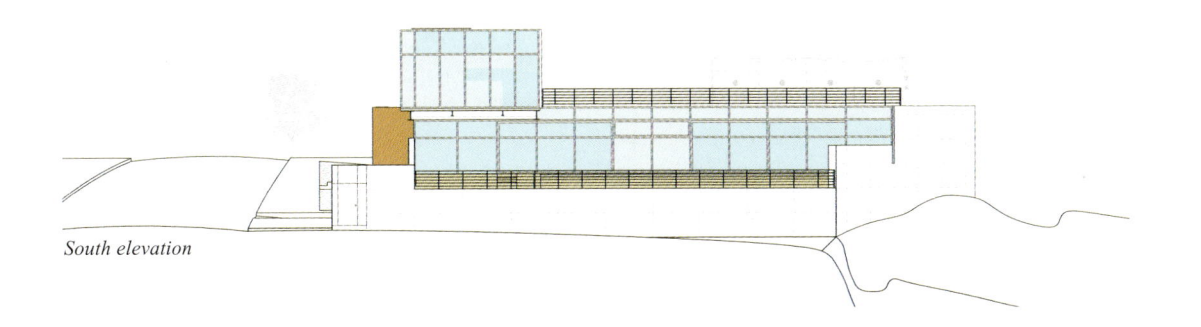

Entrance hall: looking west. Entrance on right 玄関ホール：西を見る。右に玄関

Living/dining room 居間／食堂

Entrance hall: view toward family room 玄関ホール：家族室方向を見る

Living/dining room: looking south 居間／食堂：南を見る

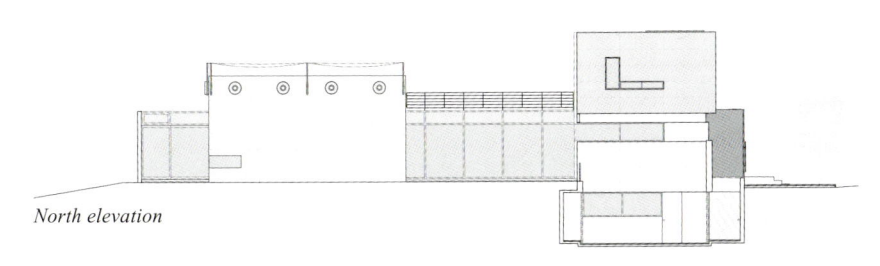

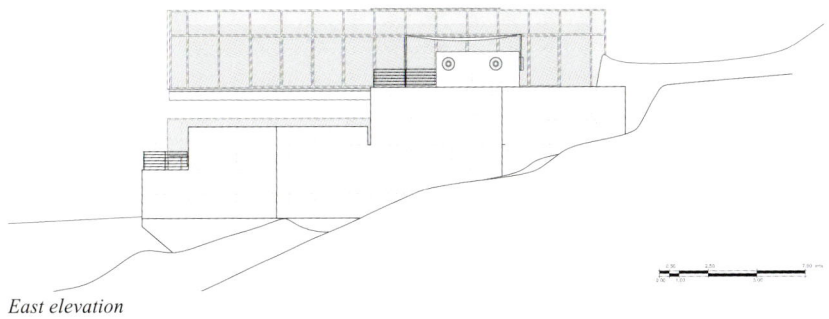

North elevation

East elevation

183

The project is located on a sloped site in the suburbs of the city of Guadalajara, with a fantastic view to the Colomos Park nearby and the city.

The house is composed by two rectangular prisms one over the other one placed in a perpendicular orientation between them. The bottom prism contains the private areas and the vestibule. At the same time, this parallelogram cuts the lot creating a private courtyard of white gravel in the highest part of the site, and a garden, a terrace and a pool in the lowest, towards the view.

The second volume, running parallel to the street, houses the public activities and floats over the place in one of its sides in a 12 meters (36 ft.) cantilever. The street elevation is clad in stone as a massive wall, while the south and west facades are glazed allowing views to the park.

In the intersection of both volumes is a double-heigh vestibule area with a skylight and a reflective pond. The lack of walls in the second floor, the use of glass for handrails and a dinning room that is hanging in a glazed mezzanine, let the space flow into the living room. The dinning room expands toward the roof of the bedrooms as a deck that becomes a wood volume defining the entrance.

グアダラハラ市郊外の斜面に建つ家からは，近くにはコロモス公園，遠くには市街が見晴らせる。

建物は，互いに直角方向に重ねた，2つの角柱状の箱で構成されている。下の方の箱にはプライベート・エリアと前室が置かれている。同時に，この平行四辺形は，敷地を切り分けて，一番高い場所には白い砂利を敷いたプライベートな中庭，一番低い場所には眺めに向いた庭，テラス，プールをつくりだす。

道路と平行する2つ目のヴォリュームにはパブリック・スペースが置かれ，その一辺は，片持ちで12メートル（36フィート）突き出し，敷地上に浮かんでいる。道路側立面は石で覆われ，マッシヴな壁を構成し，南と西側の面はガラス張りで公園が見える。

2つのヴォリュームの交差部には，2層吹抜けの前室があり，スカイライトが架かり，浅い水盤が広がる。2階には壁がなく，手摺にはガラスを使い，ガラス張りのメザニンのなかに配置された食堂の空間は居間のなかに流れ込む。木のデッキがエントランスの境界をかたどり，食堂は寝室の屋根に置かれたデッキに向かって広がる。

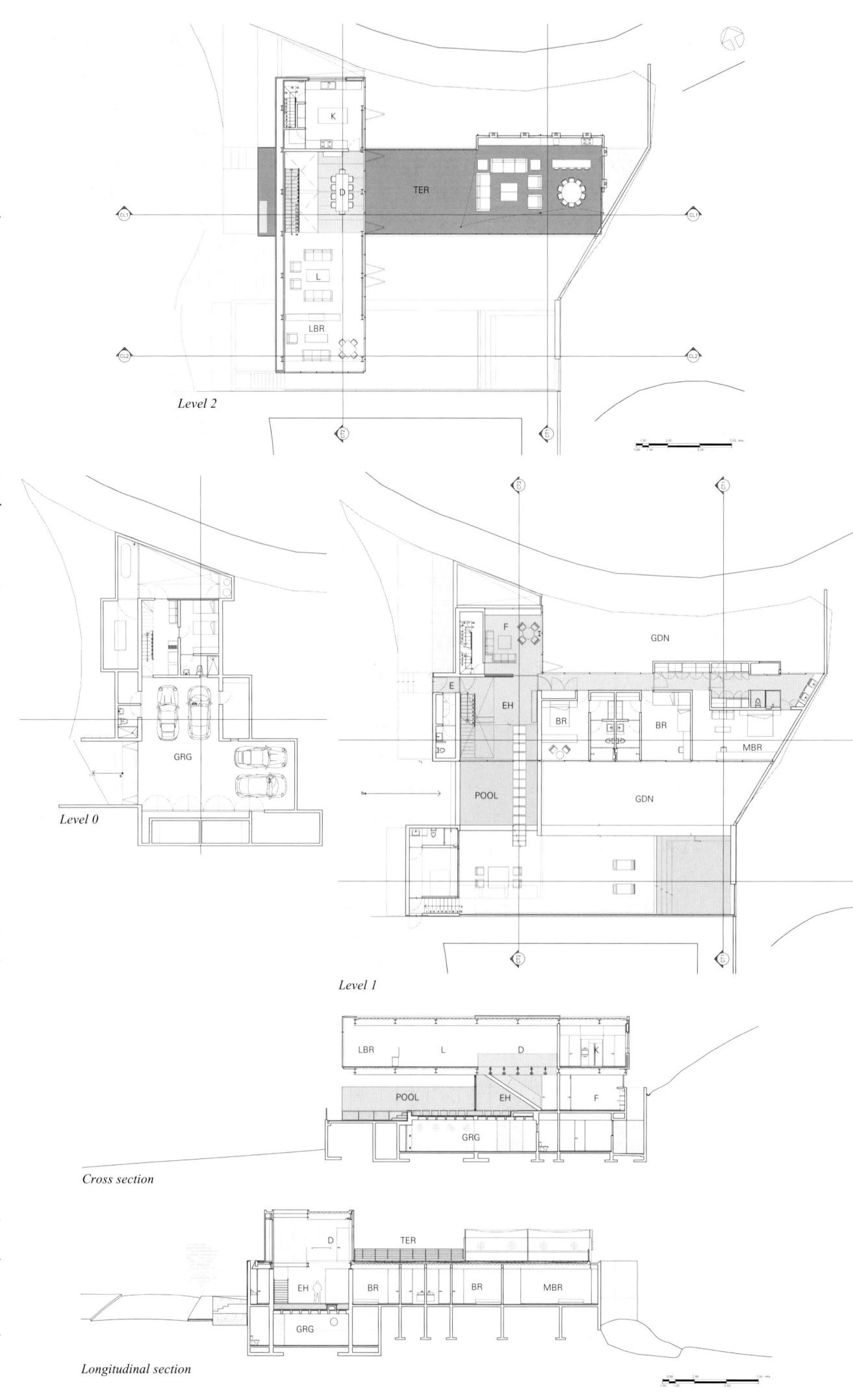

Level 2

Level 0

Level 1

Cross section

Longitudinal section

Roof terrace 屋上テラス

View toward roof terrace from dining room 食堂より屋上テラスを見る

LCM/Fernando Romero Ixtapa House

Punta Ixtapa, Zihuatanejo, Guerrero, Mexico, 2000–01

Overall view from south. Semicircular pool, fully-open living room　南側全景。半円形のプール，間口いっぱいに開口を持つ居間

Overhangs to south as eaves in smooth integration of ceiling and walls　滑らかに一体化した壁や天井は，南側に張り出し庇となる

Ground floor: looking south　1階：南を見る

Terrace on ground floor　1階テラス

Located to the northeast part of the state of Guerrero, 250 km up the cost from Acapulco via highway no. 200.
- Longitude 101.33 west. Latitude 17.38 north.

This beach is situated at the Pacific Ocean with a salinity level of 34 ppm.

The climate is melting to hot, and mid humid with heavy rains at night in summer time and in part of the autumn, in winter is the dry time, average temperature is 26ºC, and the highest levels in summer go up to 32ºC and in winter to 30ºC. Sunshine is clear almost every day of the year.

Vegetation at Ixtapa Zihuatanejo is diverse, the flower species are grouped in types of vegetation in tropical forest as sudcaducifolio and its basic characteristics is that half of their species conserve the green color even in the driest times.

Private Beach with maximum depth of 40/80 feet and an average water temperature of 24ºC, during the summer time it can rise to 32ºC, while during the winter it can drop to 21ºC, currents are moderate and there is a good quantity of sea life.

Ixtapa means in Nahuatl ëwhite sand placeí, and since 1972 is a well planned tourist development.

Ixtapa has 35 hotels, 4,203 rooms, 4 shopping centers, 2 golf courses, 1 International Airport and one port with 600 spaces. Every year 370,000 tourists go to Ixtapa.

Punta Ixtapa: residential development with lots from 3,500 m², villas and apartments, designed by Diego Villaseòor, architect.

The rules of the development force you to built a very traditional house with materials like stones and natural colors. It is also needed to have a palapa roof or at least a tejado.

The house is divided in two conditions: public and private space. The first is contained by a solid mass that holds the services like the kitchen, torment room (the family gathers when it storms), and restrooms. And the second one is on the upper floor and it has five almost identical rooms with three different kinds of bathrooms.

The concept comes from a surface that while blending on its side defines the differences between public and private.

The house has been designed to spend, with a numerous family, beach days and contemplation in this extraordinary site.

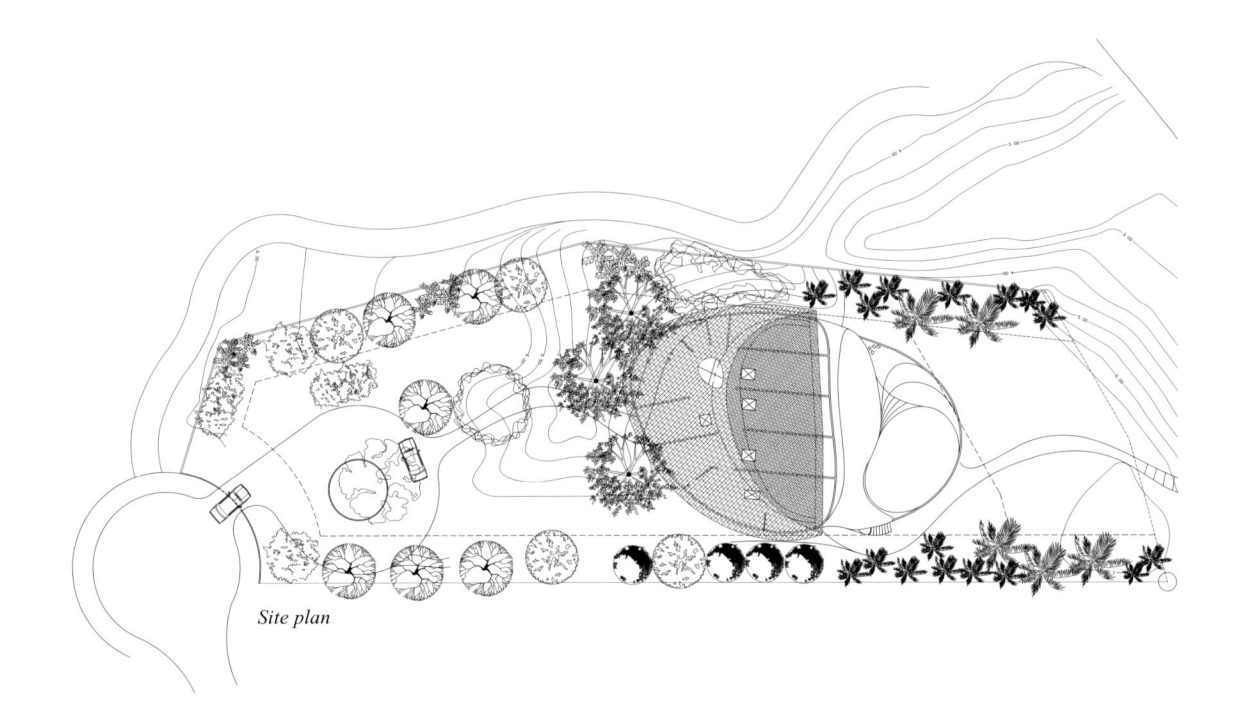

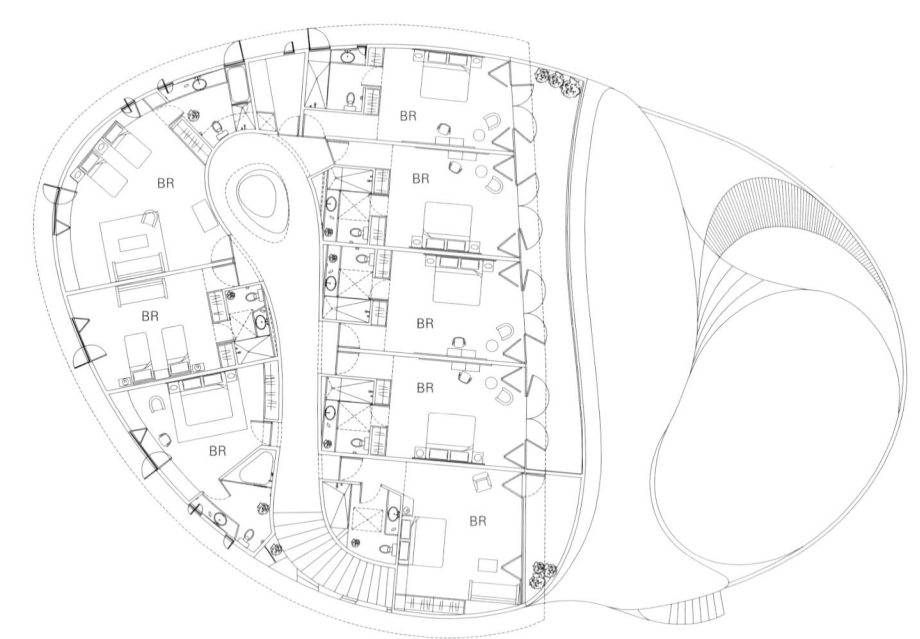

Site plan

First floor

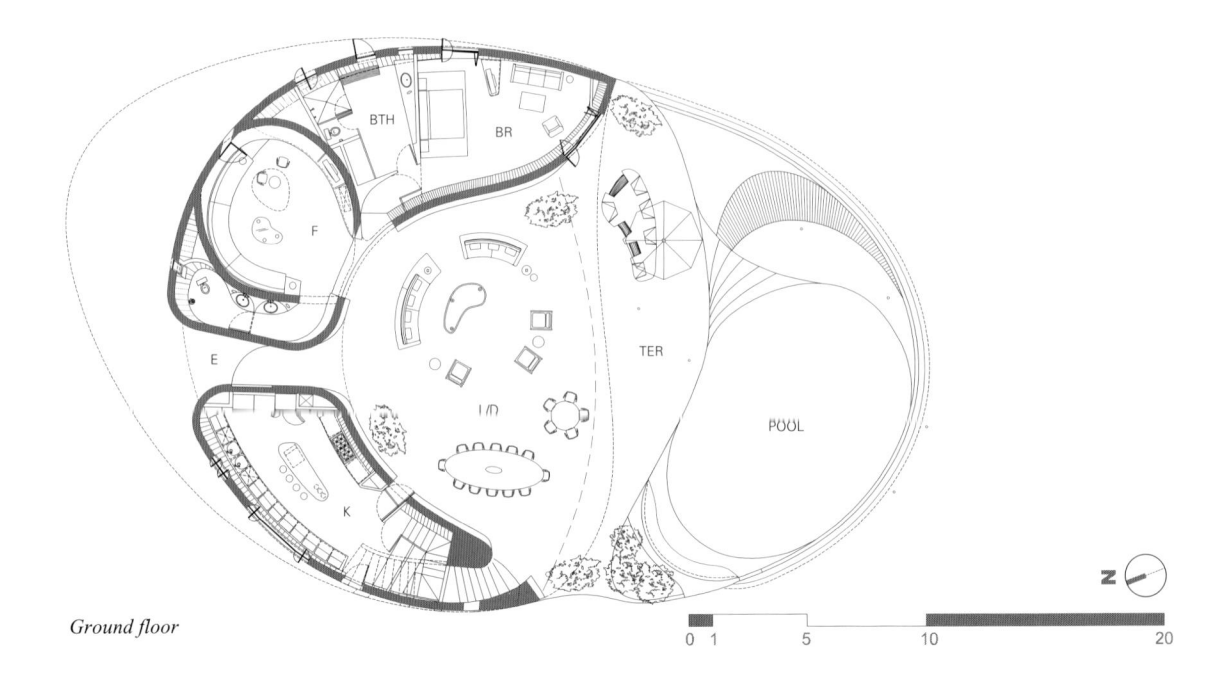

Ground floor

Family room 家族室

建物のあるイスタパは、ゲレロ州北東部、アカプルコから、ハイウェイ200号線を海岸沿いに250キロ北上した場所にある。
・西経101.33度。北緯17.38度。
この海岸は太平洋に面し、塩分濃度は34ppm。

気候は、夏と秋の一時期は溶けそうに暑く湿気もあり夜激しい雨が降るのだが、冬は乾期となる。標準気温は摂氏26度、夏の最高気温は32度を超え、冬の最高気温は30度を超える。陽射しは年間を通してほとんど毎日、澄み渡っている。

イスタパ・シウアタネホの植生は多様であり、花々は南国の落葉樹がつくる熱帯林の植生のなかに群生し、その種の半分が最も乾燥の激しい時期でさえ緑色を保つことが主要な特徴となっている。

プライベート・ビーチの水深は最大40／80フィート、海水の標準温度は摂氏24度で、夏は32度まで上がることがあり、冬は21度まで下がることがある。潮流は穏やかで、豊かな海の生物に恵まれている。

イスタパはアステカの言葉であるナワトル語で"白い砂の場所"を意味し、1972年以来、観光地としてよく計画された開発が行われてきた。

イスタパには、ホテルが35軒（総計4,203室）、ショッピングセンター4つ、ゴルフコース2つ、国際空港1つ、600艘が停泊可能なヨットハーバーが1つある。毎年37万人の観光客が訪れる。

プンタ・イスタパは、建築家ディエゴ・ビヤセールの設計による住宅開発地で、敷地は3,500平方メートル、ヴィラとアパートメントで構成されている。

開発地内の建築規制は、石のような材料、自然の色彩を使った非常に伝統的な住宅を建てることを要求している。また、藁葺きか、少なくとも瓦屋根とすることが必要である。

この住宅はパブリックとプライベート、2つの空間に分割されている。パブリックは切れ目なく続く厚いマッスに包まれ、キッチン、ファミリー・ルーム、洗面所などのサービス関係の諸室がある。プライベートは、上階にあり、ほとんど相似形の部屋5つと、それぞれに違うデザインの浴室3つがある。

コンセプトは、表面（サーフェス）という考えから生まれているが、一方で、その面はパブリックとプライベートの違いを明快に見せている側面と融合して行く。

大勢の家族が共に海岸での日々を過ごし、この素晴らしい土地で瞑想にふけることができる、そんな家を想定してデザインした。

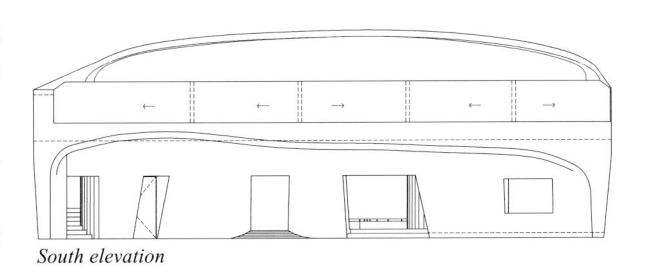

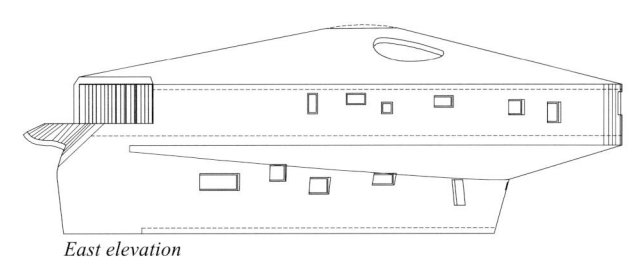

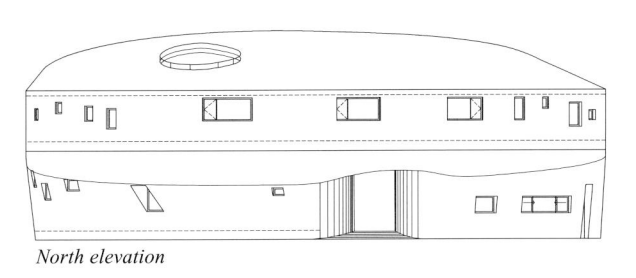

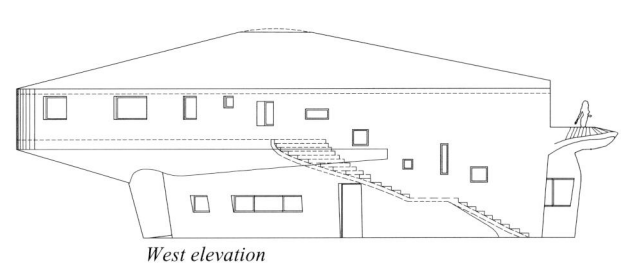

South elevation

East elevation

North elevation

West elevation

North entrance　北側エントランス

View toward Ixtapan Sea over pool　プール越しにイスタパの海を見る

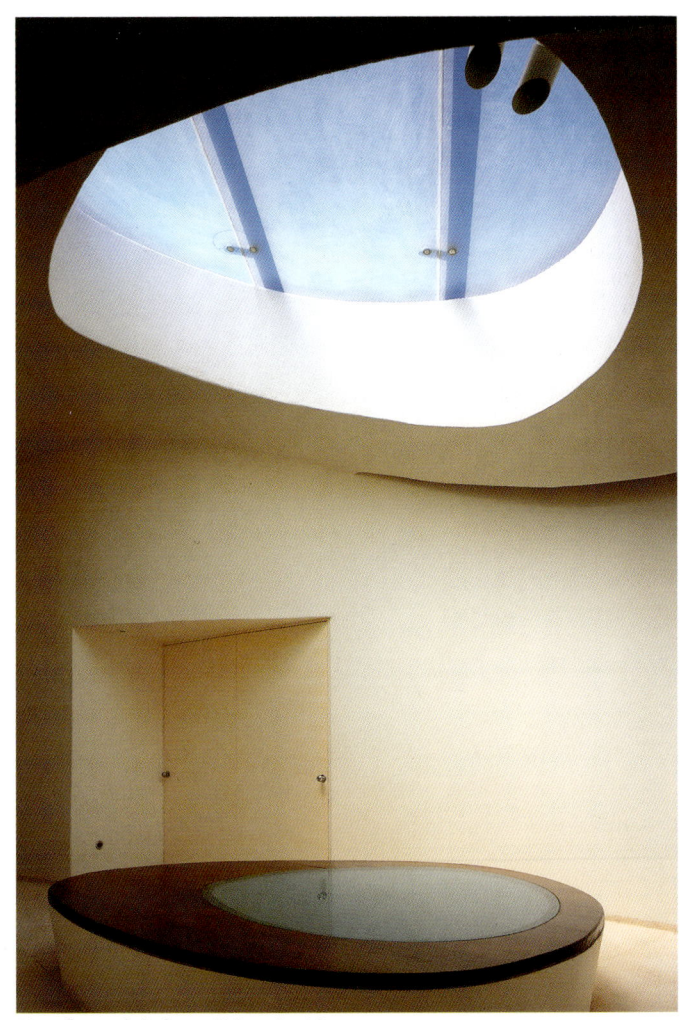

First floor: skylight　2階トップライト

View toward living/dining room: family room on right　居間／食堂を見る：右に家族室

First floor: south terrace along bedrooms　2階：寝室に沿った南側テラス

Bedroom on first floor　2階寝室

191

Michel Rojkind PR House

Tecamachalco, Mexico, 2002–04

Located in Tecamachalco estado de México, on a hillside over looking Bosques de Reforma, a remodelation and an addition was required to an existing late 60's house.

Since the client bought the house for its distribution the existing house was carefully cleaned leaving bigger and better areas, then a new part of the program was required, an independent apartment for the client's daughter.

Once entered the garage the house divides into 2 separate entrances leaving total independence to the addition which is accessed through a spiraling staircase 2 flights up.

Resembling a ballet dance composed of 2 bodies in motion, the looping sensual forms that changes angles coming out of every curve was inspired by the ballet dancer who is going to inhabit it.

Once you arrive at the apartment, it is separated in 2 half levels, the first containing the kitchen dining and living area then half flight down the TV room and the master bedroom. Taking advantage of the roof of the existing house and its skylight this roof becomes a terrace with the remaining of the chipped lava rocks used for the main wall of the house, the skylights become acrylic stools, benches and chaise lounge that change color with a led system inside. A selection of prehispanic organ plants is made to add a touch of vegetation giving this area a lunar feel.

メキシコシティの周辺部にあるメヒコ州テカマチャルコの町。緑に包まれた住宅地ボスケス・デ・レフォルマを見晴らす丘の斜面に建つ、60年代終わりにつくられた既存住宅を改造し増築を行なった。

クライアントは既存住宅の配置状況を気に入って購入したので、内壁などを細心に取り去り、前より広く快適なエリアを構成するように改造した。その後、新たに、娘のための独立したアパートの増築を依頼された。

ガレージに入ると、2つのエントランスに分かれ、2連の螺旋階段を上がって入る増築部は母屋から完全に切り離されている。

2人の身体の動きで構成されるバレエのように、カーブごとに角度を変え、官能的にループする形は、そこに住むことになるバレリーナから触発されたものである。

アパートは半階ずらして組み合せた対のブロックで構成され、エントランスを入った最初のレベルはキッチン、ダイニング、リビング、半階降りるとTV室と主寝室がある。母屋の屋根とスカイライトを利用して、この屋根の上には建物の主要な壁に使われている砕いた火山岩の残りでテラスをつくり、スカイライトは、内側からの照明によって色が変わるアクリル製のスツール、ベンチ、寝椅子に作り替えた。プレヒスパニック固有の植物を選んで配し、このエリアに月のような趣を添えた。

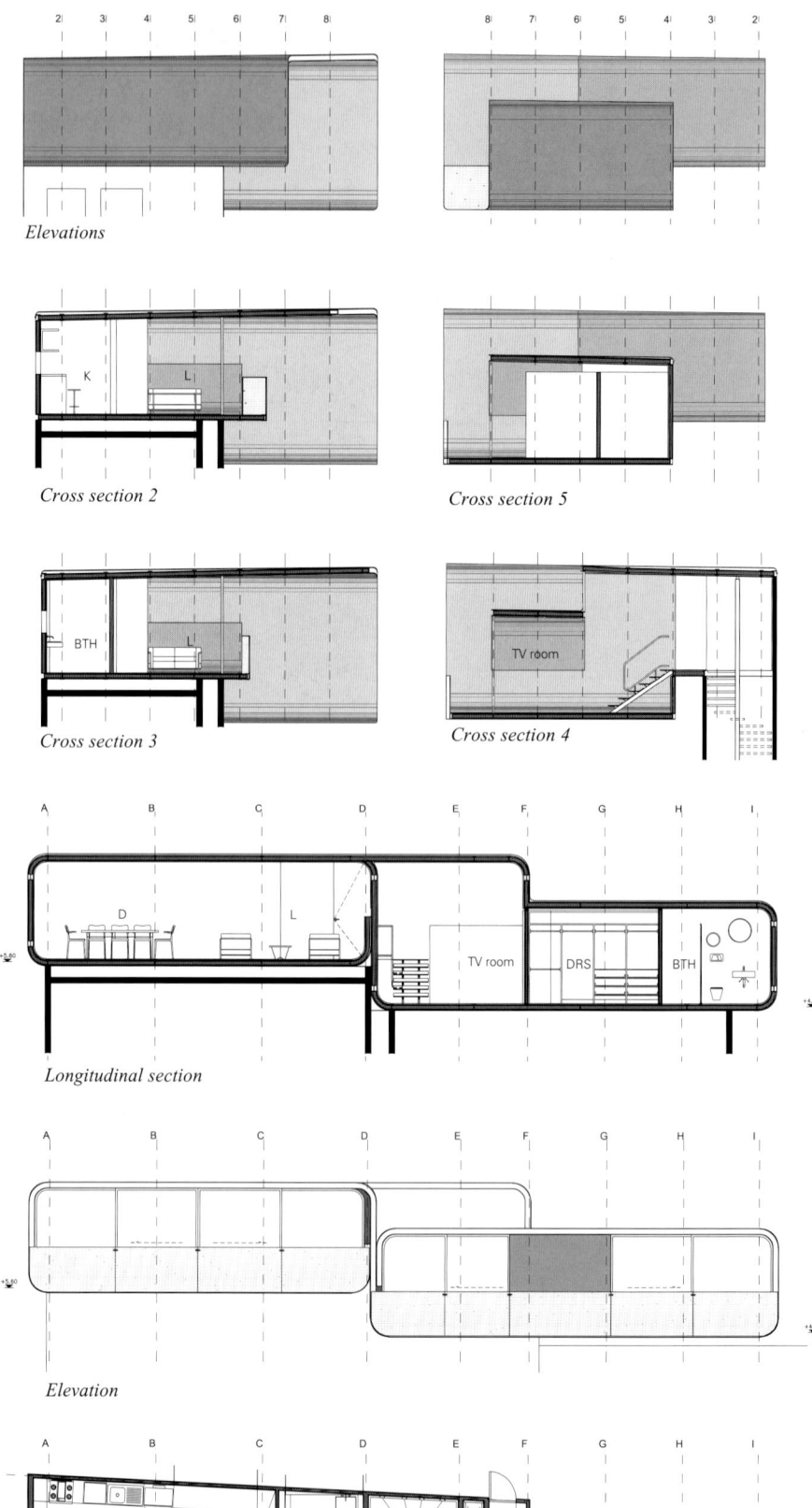

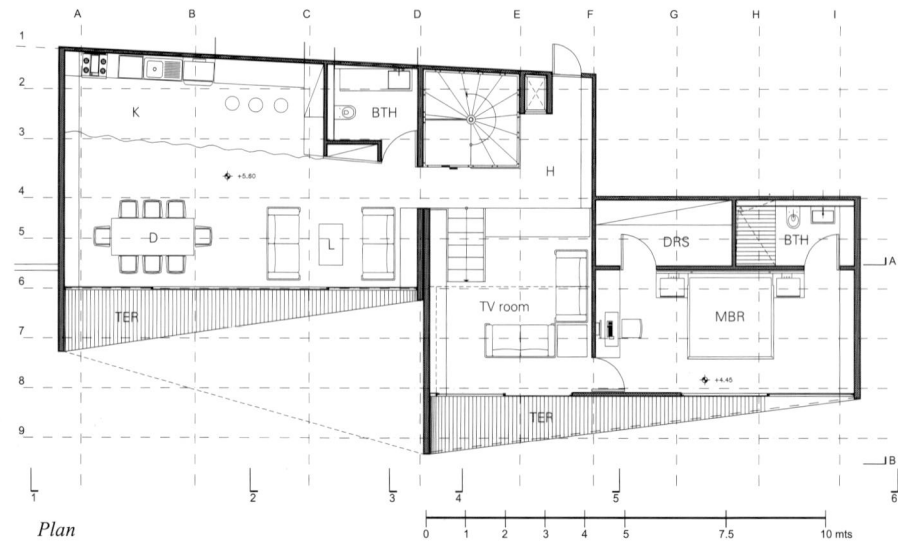

Elevations

Cross section 2

Cross section 5

Cross section 3

Cross section 4

Longitudinal section

Elevation

Plan

Existing house (below) and new appartment (above)　既存住宅（下）と新築部分（上）

New apartment: view from roof of existing house　新築部分：既存住宅の屋根より見る

Roof terrace: existing skylights covered by acrylic stools ルーフテラス：アクリル製のスツールが被せられた既存のスカイライト

TV room on right 右はテレビ室

Opening of TV room　テレビ室の開口部

TV room: looking south　テレビ室：南を見る

TV room: view toward north. Continuous ceiling, wall and flooring are made of chip board　テレビ室：北を見る。連続する天井，壁や床はチップボード製

Living/dining room　居間／食堂△▽

Felipe Leal Galeana 71

San Angel, Mexico City, Mexico, 2006–07

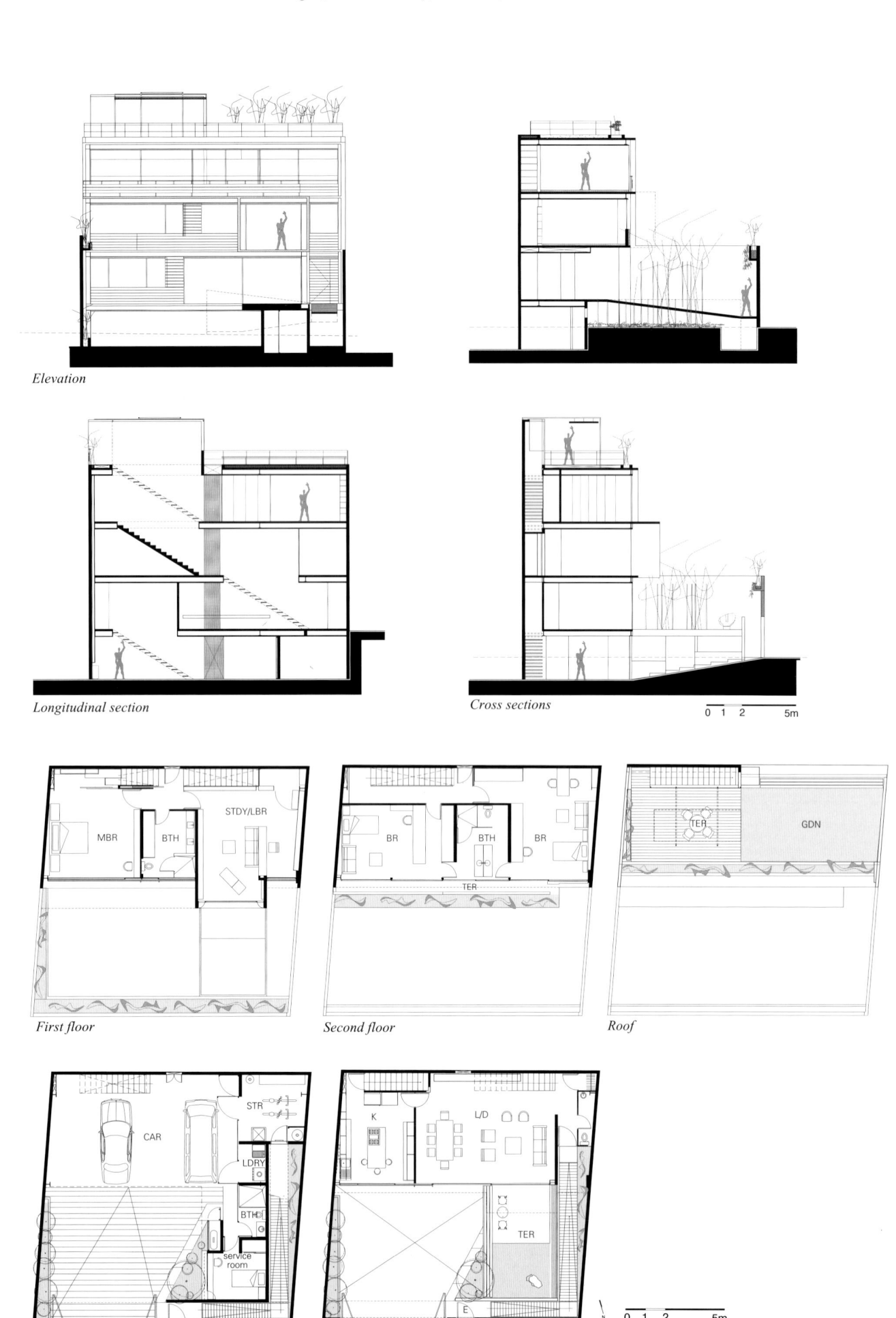

Elevation

Longitudinal section

Cross sections

First floor

Second floor

Roof

Basement

Ground floor

Galeana 71 is a familiar house located south of Mexico City on a traditional residential district with cobblestone narrow streets, the fact that confers the site an identity of typical districts that surrounded the city since XVI century that were absorbed because of the city growth during XX century.

In a 196 m² small lot (13.8 m x 13.8 m) is located the three level house and the basement that occupies only 50% of the lot, the vertical scheme of the house located on the back of the lot separates it from the street achieving privacy, silence and obtaining an intermediate space between the house and street, accomplishing a correct orientation towards the south.

Due to family configuration the activities were ordered in different levels, the basement lodges the parking area and services of the house, the ground floor which is also the entrance has public and coexistence spaces like living room, dining room and kitchen, the solution of this level act as an integrated pavilion that links directly the inside with the outside and vice versa. It is a level that takes advantage of the visual tensions and the perspectives accomplishing a bigger visual proportion.

The parents occupy the first level, the only two areas are the main room and library that are linked together, the particular shape of the library extends to the outside courtyard with a cantilevered bucket volume which purpose is to show the ideas of knowledge and music. The second level corresponds to the youth, two men of 20 and 18 years old those study and share common spaces.

The house is finished off by a roof garden that makes possible the outdoors coexistence and allows observing and enjoying the view of hills and volcanoes that surround the Valley, this roof garden idea is not only for living or contemplation but for an environmental purpose recovering the green area lost when was built the house, and helping to avoid solar reflection and promoting a green skyline creating a more pleasant place.

Analogically this is a kind of drawer-house occurs from the stratification of the family activities only mixed together in the common activities that develops in roof garden and the ground floor (public area). The neutrality of colors and little variants of materials reinforce natural and artificial light do what it corresponds to volumes modeling it. The election of the wood in the facade has the purpose to associate it with the domestic typology, the idea of a house and home as the urban refuge that offers a comfortable dwelling.

ガレアナ71は，メキシコ・シティ南部の，舗装用の小さな丸石であるコブルストーン敷きの狭い通りがある伝統的な住宅地区に位置する，親しみやすい住宅である。この敷地には，16世紀から街を取り囲み，やがて20世紀には街の発展によって吸収されていったという，地区特有のアイデンティティを持つ歴史的背景がある。

13.8メートル四方（196平方メートル）の小さな区画に，敷地面積の50％しか占めていない地上3階と地下1階建ての住宅が配置されている。敷地の後方で展開する垂直方向の建築計画は，南への的確な方位を得ながら，プライバシーと静寂を獲得しつつ，住宅と道路の間に中間的な空間をつくり出し，この住宅を道路から隔離している。

家族構成により，各機能は，それぞれ異なる階に配置された。地階には，駐車場とサービスルームが含まれている。地上階には玄関があり，リビングルーム，ダイニングルーム，キッチンといったパブリックスペースと共用スペースがある。地上階での設計手法は，内部を外部へと直接結び付け，また，その逆に，外部を内部へと直接結び付ける一体的なあずまやとしての役割をもたらしている。地上階は，より大きい視覚的調和を得ながらも，視覚的緊張感と眺望を実に巧みに利用しているのである。

両親は，互いに繋げられた主寝室と書斎という，二つのエリアだけがある2階を使用している。書斎の際立った形態は，知識と音楽に対する思想を示すキャンティレバー状のバケツ型ヴォリュームで，外部のコートヤードへと伸びている。3階は，20歳と18歳の二人の息子達のための場所である。彼らは学生で，共用スペースを一緒に使用している。

屋上は，外部との共存を実現し，谷を取り巻いている丘と火山の景色を観察したり楽しむことを可能にする屋上庭園となっている。ここでの屋上庭園の考え方は，生活や瞑想のためだけにあるのではなく，この住宅の建設によって失われた緑地を埋め合わせることや，太陽光の反射を遮るための補助となることである。また，より心地よい場所を創造しながら屋上緑化を促進することといった環境的な意図も含んでいる。

各層の家族のアクティビティが，屋上庭園やパブリックエリアである1階でのみ混じり合う，引き出し型住宅のようなものである。ニュートラルな色彩と材料の種類の少なさは，自然光と照明がヴォリュームの立体感を表現しながら調和させる，という効果をもたらしている。ファサードの木立は，住宅のタイポロジーと結び付くように意図されている。都市の隠れ処としての住まいと家庭に対する意識は，快適な住宅施設を提供することにある。

South elevation 南面

Street view 道路より見る

Terrace テラス

Living/dining room 居間／食堂

Living/dining room　居間／食堂

Study on first floor　2階書斎

Living/dining room　居間／食堂：西を見る

Kitchen　台所

Master bedroom on left　左に主寝室

View from roof garden toward terrace　ルーフ・ガーデンよりテラスを見る

Bedroom on second floor　3階寝室

Roof terrace　ルーフ・テラス

Key to Abbreviations

ALC	alcove	CLK	cloak	GDN	garden	MBTH	master bathroom	SLP	sleeping loft
ARCD	covered passageway	CT	court	GRG	garage	MECH	mechanical	SNA	sauna
ART	art room	D	dining room	GRN	greenhouse	MLTP	multipurpose room	STD	studio
ATL	atelier	DEN	den	GST	guest room	MSIC	music room	STDY	study
ATR	atrium	DK	deck	GZBO	gazebo	MUD	mud room	ST	staircase/stair hall
ATT	attic	DN	stairs-down	H	hall	OF	office	STR	storage/storeroom
AV	audio-visual room	DRK	darkroom	ING	inglenook	P	porch/portico	SUN	sunroom/solarium
BAL	balcony	DRS	wardrobe	K	kitchen	PAN	pantry/larder	SVE	service entry
BAR	bar	DRW	drawing room	L	living room	PLY	playroom	SVYD	service yard
BK	breakfast room	E	entry	LBR	library	POOL	pool/pond	TAT	tatami room
BR	bedroom	ECT	entrance court	LBY	lobby	PT	patio	TER	terrace
BRG	bridge/catwalk	EH	entrance hall	LDRY	laundry	RE	rear entry	UP	stairs-up
BTH	bathroom	EV	elevator	LFT	loft	RT	roof terrace	UTL	utility room
BVD	belvedere/lookout	EXC	exercise room	LGA	loggia	SHW	shower	VD	void/open
CAR	carport/car shelter	F	family room	LGE	lounge	SIT	sitting room	VRA	veranda
CH	children's room	FPL	fireplace	LWL	light well	SHOP	shop	VSTB	vestibule
CEL	cellar	FYR	foyer	MAID	maid room	SKY	skylight	WC	water closet
CL	closet/walk-in closet	GAL	gallery	MBR	master bedroom	SL	slope/ramp	WRK	work room

HOUSES IN MEXICO
〈メキシコの住宅〉

2008年9月25日発行

企画・編集	二川幸夫
撮影	GA photographers
英訳	谷理佐，佐藤圭，ピーター・ボロンスキー　他
和訳	菊池泰子，常石憲彦，吉村香苗　他
ロゴタイプ・デザイン	細谷巖
発行者	二川幸夫
印刷・製本	図書印刷株式会社
発行	エーディーエー・エディタ・トーキョー
	東京都渋谷区千駄ヶ谷3-12-14
	TEL. (03) 3403-1581(代)

禁無断転載

ISBN 978-4-87140-491-4 C1052